Rhapsody
of the
Hummingbird

Rhapsody
of the
Hummingbird

By Raisa Premysler

Rhapsody of the Hummingbird
© 2021 Raisa Premysler

Published by
Winged Wonders

ISBN: 978-0-578-31373-3

Cover and interior design by Jenny Kimura. Cover art: Paper texture © YamabikaY/Shutterstock.com; green watercolor drips © Anastasiya Bleskina/Shutterstock.com; hummingbird watercolor © Maria Stezhko /Shutterstock.com; honeysuckle watercolor © Marina Grau/Shutterstock .com; monarch butterfly © suns07butterfly/Shutterstock.com. Interior art: hummingbird watercolor © Romjan/Shutterstock.com; watercolor brushstroke © CreateAeon/Shutterstock.com; paper texture © YamabikaY /Shutterstock.com; watercolor background © LaLoba/Shutterstock.com.

Editing and design services provided by Indigo: Editing, Design, and More. www.indigoediting.com

Printed in the United States of America.

This book is dedicated to my loving parents and grand-parents, who gave me everything they could with lots of love. They very effectively (and I know it was terribly hard) shielded me from the sometimes ugly truth of life. I am very grateful for that.

To my children and grandchildren whom I love more than I can ever say!

And this book is for you, my love, Isaak! In your own quiet way, you produced a symphony with a loud crescendo of love. It is in all of us and is still playing every minute of every day! You are and always will be an irreplaceable composer and conductor of that beautiful music of love!

CONTENTS

Preface

A story of love, loss, laughter,
Happiness and sadness,
Friendship and bitterness.
Hope, joy, and disappointments,
Incredible beauty and ugly lies,
Great wisdom and absolute ignorance,
Mysterious butterflies and awesome, special hummingbirds!
This is a life story!

1

MATRIARCH

THE YEAR IS 1916. CZAR'S RUSSIA IS BURNING IN THE UPCOMING REVOLU-
tionary unrest, bitter winter cold, hunger, and pogroms!

A beautiful fourteen-year-old is at home by herself in the
small village of Bershad, Vinnytsia Oblast (a small *shtetl*, as we call
it in Yiddish) in Ukraine. She is trying to make the best out of a
very difficult situation and help her mother (who is at the market
with her younger sister, Rosa, trying to buy one or two frozen
potatoes to ease the raging hunger). The girl is too grown up for
her age (her father died when she was four years old, and then
her stepfather died shortly after). Her mother is struggling with
two girls during an extremely difficult time! All of that makes a
person grow up really fast.

The girl is tall and beautiful with light-brown hair in a long
braid, hazel eyes, and an incredible smile. She's wearing an old

dress, which was made and remade from other old dresses. Poor but beautiful nevertheless.

She is by the brick stove trying to create a meal for three from one last frozen potato. She is holding a long metal fire stick, which she uses to keep the fire going under the pot with mainly water, one potato and a piece of onion. The fire also helps her to stay warm.

Suddenly there's a loud noise at the door, and the door flies open. An extremely drunk Cossack actually falls inside the house. He stumbles toward the young girl, breaking cups and plates at the table (the very few possessions that this family has). He swears loudly.

The young girl's heart is racing so fast and beating so loudly that she is barely able to breathe! Thump, thump, thump. The fear paralyzes her, but she is feverishly thinking, *What to do? What to do!* Fear envelops her, but in spite of that, she understands that she needs to defend herself somehow!

Cossacks are pretty much the leftovers of the White Army, or frequently just a group of anarchistic bandits who do a "shaking up" or, as it is called, a pogrom—disorderly conduct that involves breaking and destroying property and often beating people. Occasionally they also rape and murder. They frequently target Jewish homes, which are easily identified by a mezuzah hanging at the doorpost. Usually they roam in groups of bandits, but this one is by himself, as he is probably too drunk and has lost his group. The young girl's heart and mind are racing... She is holding a long and hot fire stick, as she has just turned over the coal in the stove.

The Cossack stumbles toward her saying how beautiful she is as he unzips his pants and exposes his privates. Decisions, decisions... The teenager takes the hot metal stick, and when the hooligan is within one meter of her, she stabs him repeatedly with all her strength and all her might right into his privates. He drops to the floor violently screaming in pain, and the girl runs past him and storms out of the house. She begins to run, run, run... Her heart is about to jump out of her chest, but she keeps running. She doesn't feel the bitter cold, just fear. She turns around to see the bandit in pursuit. She runs faster and faster. Looking again, she sees him fall in a ditch by the road.

She continues to run until she is in the forest on the outskirts of the village. She hides in a tree stump and stays there until it gets dark. She is so cold now that she cannot feel her toes, and her hands feel like a solid chunk of ice. She gets up and tries to walk home. When she walks into the house, her mom begins to cry—from the broken dishes and blood stains, her mother was fearing the worst! So those are happy tears of survival, victory, and being alive! The girl's mother, Sura Berdichevsky, wraps her in the only blanket they have and gives her boiling water to drink. Surka tells her that when she came back from the market and found the door open and blood stains on the floor, she was sure that her daughter was dead. Mom was heartbroken before but now so happy to see her daughter alive!

That brave girl was my young grandmother, Khasya Grosman, who truly was our family matriarch!

2

MY GRANDFATHER—
CHANCES AND CHOICES

MY GRANDFATHER ITZHAK GENDLER WAS THE OLDEST OF SIX SIBLINGS (three brothers and three sisters). I remember that very smart, quiet, and always meticulously dressed man for his ability to reason well, for giving me a glimpse at the forbidden (which at the time was religion in Russia), and most of all for his beautiful ability to see the best in people and to wish the best to them. I think that my grandpa invented the phrase that we know now by Martin Luther King Jr.: "Hate cannot drive out the hate; only love can do that." That is how I was taught by him. He always taught me not to get angry at anything or anybody. And if I felt bad and wanted to swear at somebody, he taught me to say instead, "I do wish you well." Just something nice! He was just a very righteous person!

He also was very smart, naturally smart. He did not have much education, and he worked as a barber, but people from the whole village would come to ask him for advice like people asking their elder in the tribe or in the church. Also just recently I learned from one of my aunts (after I shared with her about my trip to Argentina and my amazement at how many fur stores they have) that some variation of me could have been on that continent??? She told me that my grandpa's family was very poor and his father (my great-grandfather), Josef, in the late 1800s or early 1900s left his wife, Zlota, and six kids and went to Argentina to make some money to try to lift his family out of poverty. He spent three years working as a fur and leather coat maker and earned enough money to bring his family out of Ukraine. He returned to Ukraine after three years just to do that, to bring them to Argentina for a better life, but both he and his wife became sick with typhus. She recovered, but he died from it.

So then my grandfather Itzhak, being the oldest, had to help his mother with his younger siblings. At a very young age, he became a barber and helped his mother with the other kids. He also was drafted and participated in World War I. He survived. Then he met my beautiful grandma at a dinner somewhere. She was eighteen; he was twenty-six. Love at first sight! That was in 1920.

Shortly after, they got married and had four kids (two girls and two boys). One of the girls was my mother, beautiful Anya/Anna.

As I mentioned previously, my grandfather gave me my first exposure to Judaism, which he practiced daily in spite that religion (any religion) was banned as forbidden and "opium for the brain." As a child, I watched my grandpa praying two to three times a day (upon awakening and before and after each meal). Before he would put on his kippah (a head covering) and tallit (ritual shawl), he would close all the curtains and make sure that none of the neighbors or passersby could see him, and then he would pray, and I would watch and be fascinated even though I did not understand anything that he was saying.

I was a very curious child and often asked him what something means, etc.... His reply was always the same: "You don't need to know. It will get in the way or even could hurt you." The forbidden fruit is always sweet, and I REALLY wanted to know! But even though I did not learn the Hebrew language that he prayed in or the meaning of the prayers, the experience of just observing him taught me a great deal of respect for beliefs (I mean any beliefs) and gave me the desire to learn. That was my glimpse at the FORBIDDEN! There is a whole other chapter to my grandpa's life which I didn't know until I got married, but that is a story for another chapter...

My grandpa Itzhak Gendler passed away on March 13, 1967, when I was fourteen years old. He hated the month of March and was superstitious about the number thirteen, and that is when he died! I saw him in a coffin with his tallit (shawl), Talmud (prayer book), and kippah (head covering), all of which went with him to the grave!

It was almost twenty years later when I rediscover all that and was free to learn and understand what he did. It had been fifty-three years since he died, and for at least the last forty, I always said Kaddish (a memorial prayer for those who have gone to their eternal home). I recited Kaddish for my grandpa every year on the anniversary of his death and lit a yahrzeit (memorial) candle. He would've liked it!

Another interesting memory is when I watched him listen to the news and he would get upset and bitterly call them liars. That was my righteous grandfather!? That was strange and unusual for him, but all he would say was "If people go, you go too!" In the future that would help me make a very difficult and complex decision about leaving the Soviet Union!

Right before the World War II, my grandpa made (I am sure) a very difficult decision to stay at his home in Ukraine. At that time people had already heard of terrible atrocities that were happening in Poland and other places in Europe, and all of his siblings and their families had been evacuated to the Far East of Russia. He stayed! As a believer in the good in people, he said that people who have such beautiful composer, music, and culture could not kill! He ended up in a ghetto in Ukraine with his four kids, barely survived, and lost his two sons—Josef, age eighteen, and Lazar, age thirteen, of blessed memory!

That was precisely why he said, actually commanded us: "If people go, you go!" That started ringing very loudly in 1974 through 1976 when over fifty thousand Soviet Jews per year started their exodus from the Soviet Union. Yes, Grandpa, even after your death, you were leading us. You planted the seed!

3

A FAMILY LEGEND AND
FAMILY SECRETS

WHEN YOU FIRST LOOK, IT IS A USUAL STORY—"BOY MEETS GIRL..." THEY both lived in a small village in Ukraine. They both grew up poor. There was a nine-year difference between them, so they didn't mingle much growing up. The man, Itzhak, was good-looking, and at the time when this story began (around 1920), he was a quite mature age of twenty-seven. She, Khasya, was barely eighteen, and both were having dinner at a neighbor's house.

Khasya was a natural beauty, tall with a long braid of a very light brown/sand color and beautiful hazel eyes. Itzhak saw the young lady, and he was instantly in love! She smiled back at him, and then they met again and again, and probably a few months later, Itzhak asked Khasya's mother for the girl's hand in marriage! They got married in September of 1920, and exactly nine months later, their first daughter was born on May 30, 1921, and they named her Manya/Maria. Then three years later a second daughter arrived, and they named her Anna/Anya, in a Russian version of the name. She was born on the coldest day of the year, January 21, 1924. That was also the day that Lenin died and the whole country was crying. My grandpa, Itzhak, wasn't very happy with a second girl being born. He really wanted a son! When he heard the news of a second daughter just being born, he was on his way home in a rather gloomy mood. Poverty, hunger, and another mouth to feed, and it was a girl?... But then as I said, the whole country was in mourning for Lenin, who passed away that very day. Itzhak walked home and found a wallet on the ground by the market. The money inside allowed him to buy two bags of flower and a bag of potatoes! That made his day, and the news of my mother's arrival wasn't so bad after all.

After Anya, two boys arrived, Josef in 1926 and Lazar/Lenya in 1928, respectively. Should I say they lived happily ever after? But then it would be the end of the story, and it is only the beginning!

They lived in the small village of Bershad in Ukraine. He was a barber, and she was a mom to four kids by the age of twenty-six (seven, four, two, and a newborn). The family was very poor but trying to make ends meet! The young woman had an entrepreneurial streak in her (I'm not sure how she developed that, but she did). In Ukraine and in Russia in general at that time, to do any kind of business was illegal and punished with imprisonment, so only the very, very brave would attempt something like that!!!! In reality, it was straight commerce: buy cheap, sell higher, and make a profit, pretty much export/import, but not in Lenin's and later Stalin's communist RUSSIA! So the young

woman decided to do that undercover. She just wanted to supplement her family's income. It was 1930 or 1931, an awful time
of depression while hunger was rampant, and of course it was
the pre-war era! Like I said, she was a brave young lady!

In a way, she started a new business, except it wasn't called
that then. Even at such a bad time, leather coats and jackets were
very popular with Moscovites (people who lived in Moscow). She
found a family that was making them, and she would buy from
them (I guess she introduced a concept of a credit card without
knowing that...), load up two or three suitcases, and take them
on a train to Moscow where she would sell them to small stores
and individuals, making enough profit to cover all expenses and
have an additional income for herself. The family was able to
have better meals once in a while. It really worked! There were
grandmothers and several aunts (her husband was the oldest
of six and had three sisters), who all pitched in with child care
when she was gone.

Once again, in a way she established quite a business (pro-
ducers, suppliers, profit). My grandmother Khasya was also
very frugal, a good housekeeper, a great cook, and a very good
mom. Essentially she was gone three to five days once a month
and then back home. In mid to late 1934, she went on one of
her usual trips but didn't come back in a week like usual... Her
husband was concerned—rightfully so—and went to Moscow.
I'm not sure how, but he found her, and when he arrived, there
was a man in the apartment in an officer's uniform! Romance?
Unexpected new love? Love so strong, she forgot her own children???!!!!! Unbelievable, but I guess it was true...

Another child was born, a little girl, and Khasya's mom came to Moscow to help with the baby. Shortly after that, both Khasya's baby and her mother contracted typhus and died from it!!! As she struggled with grief, she became ruthless and was caught and put in prison in Moscow just as the war broke out! Horrible, big World War II.

After finding his wife with another man, the heartbroken husband went back to the village and shortly got married to an awful lady who hated kids. My mom, Anya, was only eleven years old with two brothers—Josef, 9, and Lazar/Lenya, 7. Her older sister, Manya, who was fourteen at the time, had gone to the city of Vinnytsia and lived there with a relative to attend a middle education place (like a community college that you could attend after completing eighth grade in school) to become a teacher. My mom, Anya, was forced to become a mother figure to her two younger brothers at the tender age of eleven, when most girls were playing with dolls still. The stepmother would frequently lock all three kids out in the cold, and they would sit outside shivering until their father would come home from work! As bad of a stepmother as one could get. She was plain ugly, unkempt, and not very domestic—almost never cooked.

In spite of the challenging family situation and the war and the hunger, the father and stepmother managed to have two more kids, a girl and a boy. The youngest, the boy, Volodya, died as a child from some sort of infectious disease. He was five. All through the war, the family lived in that little village, where Hitler's residence was close by. The girl's name was Dina.

Itzhak refused to evacuate (even after all of his siblings did), as he refused to believe in the evil in people. As a result, he lost his other two sons. The oldest one was a warrior, and the minute he turned eighteen (which was in 1944), he joined the army. On his first mission, the tank that he was in hit a mine and exploded, killing everyone inside. He is buried in a mass grave in East Prussia. He was only eighteen years old! The youngest brother died from meningitis at age thirteen in his sister Anya's embrace. He was a young dreamer, and as he was dying, he talked about the solar system and wondered if in the future people would get to the moon. Anya said that if he had survived, he would probably be an astronomer or space scientist. He really fantasized about other planets, space, and stars! When her father returned from work and found his son dead in Anya's embrace, he blamed her bitterly and maybe even beat her, even though it wasn't her fault. The poor teenaged Anya, missing her best young years with war, poverty, hunger, illness, and death, all without a mother's shoulder to cry on!!!!

When the war was over, Khasya was released from jail and came back to her village. Khasya and Itzhak married again, and only then did they live happily ever after until his death on March 13, 1967, at the age of seventy-four. This is the untold story of my grandfather Itzhak and my grandmother Khasya and their daughter Anya, who became my mother! Life is so beautiful but also so very complicated! You never know what is around the corner or how life can sneak up on you with twists and turns? Get ready for a wild roller-coaster ride, as it is never a straight line! Put on the seatbelt and take a ride!

I lived with my maternal grandparents until I was ten or eleven. Then when they moved to the city of Odessa, I spent every summer of my childhood there swimming in the Black Sea, eating good food my grandma cooked, and meeting multiple new relatives that I didn't know I had. I also went to movies and theater musicals with my grandma. My grandma was my best friend, my idol. She was just *cool*.

But even as a child, I noticed no warmth between my mom and grandma. But then, my mom wasn't a hugger. My dad was, and I guess I inherited that from him. My mom truly loved me and my brother, but she almost never hugged and kissed us. You could say she was emotionally reserved. Only now I begin to understand what an emotional strain both my mom, Anya, and my grandmother Khasya lived under, because I never asked. They never volunteered the information—I guess to protect me? My mom talked about how hard it had been when she was a teenager, but then it was hard for everyone in the time of war, despair, and hunger! I was young and did not ask questions when I could've and should've.

Fast-forward to my wedding day, August 25, 1973. I was twenty-one and getting married to my sweet Isaak, who was twenty-three. It was a big wedding with lots of guests, and then I saw a lady in her fifties who looked a lot like my aunt Manya. She was introduced to me as my grandfather's "other daughter." At that time, I had no knowledge of my grandmother's time away from her family, her other child, my grandfather's marriage during that time, and his other two children. To me, my grandparents were perfect. So at age twenty-one, I met an aunt I didn't know I had. What? My perfect grandpa was not as perfect as I thought? My grandpa was gone by then, but my grandma was at my wedding. I was confused, but it was my wedding day, so I still didn't touch the forbidden subject! I was too busy, and it seemed too painful to talk about.

Then my beautiful daughter was born one year and one day after our wedding, and my grandma came to the city of Vinnytsia, where we lived, to help and take care of my daughter, Lilya. I was incredibly grateful that my seventy-two-year-old grandma was leaving her comfortable home in a warm place in Odessa and coming to help me even though she had to stay with us in one room! I mentioned that to my mom, who simply replied, "She owes me that." I thought that was strange, but I still didn't ask anything.

Then my grandma at the age of seventy-nine was standing by me at the Good Samaritan hospital when I gave birth to my son! Later after we had moved to the United States, my grandmother's younger sister, Rosa (who lived in Ukraine with my parents), said to me, "Your grandma had another daughter, who died. Our mother died too in Moscow..." I still didn't ask.

My grandma lived in Portland until she was ninety-six and peacefully died in her sleep. All those years she was my grandma, but I was too busy to ask about painful details.

I pulled the story like pieces of a puzzle from single phrases, facial expressions, filling in the missing links. This was the hardest chapter for me to write. These pages scream: "Please talk to your loved ones, and do ask them about their life again and again and again!!!! When they are gone, you often wish that you would've done so, but it is just too late!"

It warms my heart to think about my grandparents because I truly loved them and they loved me, but they were human, and life happened, and they made mistakes—sometimes big, horrible mistakes but...they were just human, and life was happening...

Forgive me for not asking! I know that you are together in heaven, and the memory of you will always stay with me! You taught me some great lessons and values, and I am grateful for that! Your hard experiences and mistakes in judgment showed me your resilience and incredible willpower. May the memory of you be a blessing!

My mom also took the family secret to her grave. I guess it was too painful for her to talk about, and I did not really ask.

When she was dying in April of 2002 and she was very ill, she saw her deceased young brother Lenya/Lazar sitting next to her. She told me to go to the kitchen and get him a biscuit, as he was very hungry. Two days before she died, her brother was constantly there and, as she had done many years ago, she worried about him being hungry!!!

"Even though I walk through the valley of the shadow of death, I will fear no evil, for you are with me; your rod and your staff, they comfort me..."

4

FIRST AND ONLY LOVE

THIS IS A CHAPTER OF LOVE—BIG AND BEAUTIFUL, INNOCENT LOVE. MY chapter of meeting and falling in love with Isaak, which is a blessing from above.

I heard about Isaak first from my most trusted source, my grandma. She was my authority on everything and a great judge of character.

My cousin Josef was engaged to Isaak's sister Lisa, and Isaak came to meet my grandma and to discuss wedding arrangements for his sister. Their father was in his midseventies and in failing health, so Isaak was a stand-in for his father even though he was only twenty years old then, four years younger than his sister. He had just been discharged from the army, held a job, and took care of his parents. He was mature beyond his years as he represented the bride's family.

After that meeting, my grandma couldn't stop talking about

how mature and smart he was. She talked about him with great admiration and told me that he had a depth to his character. That really intrigued me and definitely raised my curiosity. As I said before, my grandma was very smart and a good judge of character. Now I really wanted to see him, at least a picture of him. Much later somehow I saw a picture of him taken in his military outfit with a warm fur hat on. That is the funny part of the story.

Like every teenager I was into music, especially one vocalist who had a superb voice and was very popular named Muslim Magomayev. He was my idol! My childhood friend Tanya and I were totally and completely obsessed with him. We were almost equally obsessed with the Beatles, but Muslim was one step above that on our obsession scale. We knew every song he performed by heart, followed his concerts, toasted to him every holiday, and even wore mourning clothes to school when somebody spread a rumor about his untimely death! We were so hopelessly in love with him! The only reason that I am telling you about my infatuation is because when I looked at Isaak's picture, I completely saw the face of my idol, Muslim! Instantly in love?

I had already begun to like Isaak just from my grandma talking about him, but fate did not bring us together until two years later. It was the summer of 1972. Just like every summer before, I was at my grandma's *dacha* ("summer home" in Russian, but Grandma lived there all year long)! My cousin Valya, exactly my age, was also there, and she had a group of young guys from her hometown in Ukraine, and we would all hang out together at the beach and would go out at night.

One day as we came back from the beach, there was a young man at the water pump getting some water. I said to him: "Are you the famous Isaak that I've heard so much about?" He very quietly replied, "Yes."

Apparently my cousin Josef, who was a car mechanic and chauffer, had been driving a bus from Vinnytsia to Odessa. Isaak was upset about failing some exam at Polytechnic Institute and was depressed about it. So Josef (his brother-in-law) asked him to come along and spend a few days at the Black Sea at his grandma's dacha. He did. When I first saw him, I guess that I was not in love at first sight—I was not smitten. All of us changed, rested, and left for a night on the town without even inviting him!

The next morning when we met for breakfast, Isaak said how cold it was to sleep on a bus/van, and like a complete idiot, I just blurted out that he should've asked me to come and warm him up. Playful, flirty? Maybe. I really did not even mean it? Why would I say that? Later that day we went to pick some grapes from the vine, and that is where we kissed first... The rest is history.

In the fall I went to my medical school in the city of Chelyabinsk, Ural Mountains in Russia, and in September after having strep throat that turned into rheumatic fever, I ended up in a hospital rather sick. My awesome grandma saved the day again and came to stay with me while I was in the hospital. Isaak ended up in a hospital at the same time with autoimmune arthritis. The same disease and in the hospital at the same time? Then we started a postal romance—we started writing letters, and the romance blossomed. One time after I picked up the letter from the post office where I'd walked with my grandma, I was excited, and I guess my hands were shaking. My grandma took one look and simply stated, "Yes, he is going to be your husband!"

I missed too much school and needed to have prophylactic antibiotics treatment, so I had to take an academic year off. I went home and visited Isaak in Vinnytsia. Technically, I visited my cousin, but I saw much more of Isaak than my cousin.

Isaak took me to his work, where he was in charge of constructing a huge commercial building. It was just a foundation at that time, and since I did not know anything about construction, it was not really exciting to me, but his handsome eyes were sparkling with excitement. I loved him for showing so much of his incredible deep passion for his work! Then in the spring of the next year, he came to my city of Stryi, Lviv, in Ukraine and told me that he wanted to ask my parents for my hand.

First we went to a carnival in town and he said that if he beat me in the target shooting, I should marry him. I agreed. I was good, but I lost—and I do not think intentionally. He was better in target shooting, and he honestly won!!!

On August 25, 1973, we got married, and I definitely loved Isaak then, but I did not know that our sweet love would last for forty years *and* it would become stronger and stronger every year. We truly loved each other more and more. I do not remember a single day that Isaak would come home from work and not give me a kiss. We would sit watching TV and holding hands, and our kids would frequently make fun of us doing it!? We would take a drive somewhere, and it would be silent in then car, and then one would say something and the other person would reply saying, "How did you know that I was thinking of that?" We were finishing sentences for each other. Our love grew stronger as the years passed. That love brought us *two beautiful* children, who in turn blessed us with two awesome grandkids in Isaak's lifetime, and now I am blessed with two more. Our sweet Iyla was named for Isaak.

Our love was so unbelievably beautiful, but unfortunately a terrible illness took Isaak from me when he was sixty-two and I was sixty. We had so much more to give and to receive, but I guess it was not meant to be. Isaak was and forever will be my first and last love!!! And I know that he continues to love me from heaven forever and ever. Until we meet again, my love....

I would like to end this chapter with a saying of English novelist, Sir Hugh Walpole;

"The most wonderful of all things in life is discovery of another human being with whom one's relationship has a growing depth, beauty, and joy as the year's increase. The inner progressiveness of love between two human beings is a most marvelous thing, it cannot be found by looking for it or by passionately wishing for it. It is a sort of divine accident and the most wonderful of all things in life."

5

THE MIRACLE AND BLESSING
OF BIRTH—ARRIVAL OF OUR
LUCKY CHARM!

As the story goes, Isaak and I got married on August 25, 1973. It was a beautiful and big wedding in the city of Stryi, Lviv Oblast, Ukraine. That was where my parents lived and I had grown up. It was a small town of approximately fifty thousand people in Western Ukraine with a rather significant military base. The nearby town Lviv was formerly Lemberg, and until September 17, 1939, was a Polish town. And lot of people spoke Polish when I lived there. Nationalism was very high and even though I went to a Russian-speaking school and spoke Russian at home, I needed to study Ukrainian language and literature, as you simply could not buy anything in the store if you spoke or asked in Russian.

At our wedding, we were so young. I had just turned twenty-one, and Isaak was twenty-three. We got married during my academic leave year. Technically, I was due to start my second year in my seven-year medical school, so Isaak and I flew back to Chelyabinsk in Ural Mountains in Russia, and he helped me settle in, but then he returned to his work in Vinnytsia, Ukraine. We planned for me to be in Chelyabinsk for my second year and then to try to transfer to the medical school in Vinnytsia. Life of course had other plans for us.

In order for me to return to school, I had to go through a full medical exam. I was not feeling well, but I thought that it was because I was missing Isaak and was in that frozen wonderland all by myself. During the exam, I found out that I was pregnant. The officials actually told me that I would not be allowed readmission to school until I got an abortion, their reasoning being that it was too soon after my rheumatic fever to have a child and that pregnancy was dangerous to me and the future child.

By the way, abortions at that time in Russia were the most common form of birth control. Talk about state-enforced decision on what you want to do with your body (which was done under the umbrella pretense of good medical practices). Needless to say, I spent my days going to the post office getting in one of those phone booths and crying so hard and sobbing and asking Isaak what to do. I did not want to have an abortion! So, he just said to me that I should come home and we would decide what to do.

I really was also heartbroken for my school, because it had been a hard road to get there and I'd made it and now, if I left,

I might not be able to get back into medicine. My mom told me that ever since I was five or six, all I'd wanted to do was give shots and bandage all the older neighbors sitting outside on our common balconies. All other girls were playing with dolls, but I was fascinated with my doctor's set. I always knew that that what I wanted to do was to be a doctor no matter what it took to get there.

This was after two years of disappointing tries to get into medical school in Ukraine. That was especially disappointing because I was absolutely correct on a test that was denied, and when I requested an in-person review of my admission scores, I met with a bureaucrat who brought my test that had been intentionally crossed out in red and was now unreadable!!! I did not prove anything and came into contact head-on with corruption and antisemitism.

My parents tried to tell me that it would be next to impossible to get into medical school in Ukraine, and I did not believe it. I said, "I am an honor student, straight As—of course I can get into any school I want." But after my second year of trial in Ukraine, one young girl said to me: "My mom gave a cow to the dean. How about yours?" My rose-colored glasses were taken off, and I instead flew to a very cold part of the country, where corruption and antisemitism had not penetrated the system yet!

I'd made it, but now I would have to give it up—there was no doubt in my mind that I would choose my child over my career! This decision was also reinforced by friends of mine, a beautiful couple (he was a doctor and she was a teacher). That young lady had been in her first year of college when she got pregnant and had an abortion and after that was not able to conceive again. She adamantly told me: "You will give up medicine, but you are not having an abortion!"

I left Chelyabinsk, Russia, and returned to Vinnytsia, Ukraine, where I lived with Isaak and his parents in a two-room apartment. I still had a hope to return to medical school someday and truly dedicated the nine months of my pregnancy to that! Because Chelyabinsk was in the Russian Federation and Vinnytsia in Ukraine, I needed to appeal to two different Ministries of Health (Russian in Moscow and Ukrainian in Kiev). Isaak worked in Vinnytsia as a construction engineer, and it would make all the sense in the world to let me transfer to medical school in Vinnytsia to reunite the family, but... We made multiple personal pleas in both Moscow and Kiev, but to no avail. Some of those trips were in my last months of pregnancy, very hot and uncomfortable in summer, and my very pregnant abdomen was practically sitting at the table of those officials. I asked and begged and cried, appealed to their senses, but nothing worked! I pretty much gave up on my idea of ever returning to medical school and instead concentrated on becoming a mother.

In my last month of pregnancy, I moved to stay with my parents in Stryi (that was where I had been born, and our daughter would be born there). In late August of 1974, I developed rather regular contractions and was taken to the hospital for what ended up being seventy-two hours of continuous labor (the pain and horror of that, I will spare the reader—I just want to say that if it had been here in the USA, I would have ended up having a C-section).

Finally in late August a beautiful olive-eyed girl arrived at 4:15 p.m. weighing at 8 pounds. I could recognize those beautiful big eyes on a stretcher that carried probably twenty screaming babies all wrapped in the same white wraps and white hats. They all looked the same except I could see those beautiful eyes from a distance. My beautiful flower, Lilya, was one of a kind, and she had a bruise above her right eye, which caused me a lot of worries, sleepless nights, and crying. I was reassured. This beautiful baby girl changed everything. She became my life! I even began to forget about my medical school. All I was now was a MOM!

But in the beginning of September shortly after Lilya's birth, I received a telegram stating that I had been accepted to transfer my second year of medical school to Vinnytsia at the school named for the famous surgeon, Nikolay Ivanovich Pirogov! What happened???? After so many personal pleas and constant refusal, I needed to report to school in three weeks???

Our daughter was my lucky charm then and has been my lucky charm ever since!

So now both excitement and fear enveloped me. Yes, I very much wanted to be a doctor, but how would I manage to study and care and breastfeed a one-month-old baby all at the same time?

Even though we lived with my parents-in-law, they were not able to help with child care (just too old and ill)! My grandma came to the rescue once again. She left her home in Odessa and came to live with us in our one room and sleep on a rollaway and be our live-in babysitter. That room became a bedroom for four, living room, dining room, study, and guest room. But we were happy, and even some people envied us, as we had indoor plumbing! We were young!

Breastfeeding did not go well with my busy class schedule. I had no pump and tried to pump by hand in a bathroom that was full of smoke (it was very strange, but everyone except me smoked in medical school, and you could not smoke in a classroom or hallway so everybody smoked in the restroom). No wonder breastfeeding did not work. I stopped after a month. Luckily, the Children's Kitchen, which prepared daily supplies of infant food, was good in Ukraine and Grandma took care of my sweet girl while I was in school.

After five or six months in school, I found out what happened and why I really was back in school. Before I tell you the story, I do need to explain one thing that is hard for American readers to digest. So, in spite of religion being a forbidden subject, my being a Jew was the nationality in my passport (as we would lovingly call graph 5)? Yes, as far as I was able to trace down, all my ancestors were born in Ukraine, but we never were Ukrainian. Our nationality was Jewish.

Higher education admission offered to Jews was limited to 2 percent per year. It was not based on your abilities, achievements, test scores (like SATs), etc. Just the stamp in your passport, your "nationality."

So, some people learned the ins and outs of the corrupt system and bought themselves admission to the higher education institutions. Bribery was widespread. That was the case in the medical school in Vinnytsia. This one family seeking admission for their child bribed the dean of the school. As a part of that huge bribe, the dean's wife received a full-length mink coat. Their child was admitted.

That was a year of massive emigration of Jews out of the Soviet Union directly related to increasing antisemitism! I'm not sure what the exact circumstances were for that particular family, but I learned that they emigrated to Israel and then decided to expose the corruption and discrimination in the system. They wrote a letter to the appropriate authorities, many agencies, and the press. They said to go to the dean's home and in the lining of his wife's mink coat, they would find banknotes. They even provided the banknote numbers. Needless to say, that dean was fired and suffered consequences, but as a sign of goodwill and appearing to hold "no grudges," the school needed to admit a Jew. I was that person.

However, I still think that it was our lucky charm, our sweet girl, Lilucya, who brought me back to medicine, which proved to be a big part of my life, great fulfillment, and joy!

Forty-five years later, she remains my lucky charm!!! May you always shine bright with good health, good deeds, endless love, and the goodness that you project. Fly high in life, my social butterfly! I love you forever and ever, and am so happy to dedicate this chapter to you!

6

DECISIONS, DECISIONS

IN 1974 IN THE FORMER SOVIET UNION, THE WAVE OF EMIGRATION FOR Soviet Jews reached an all-time high of fifty or sixty thousand that year! Antisemitism had been on the rise. You could easily be offended on a street by being told that you are a kike (or *zhid* in Ukrainian) and told, "Go to Israel!" My grandfather's words were echoing louder and louder: "When people go, you go too."

Do not stay behind! I was in my second year of medical school, and it was very important to me, but the anxiety of increased emigration and the bitter taste of antisemitism made me almost ruthless. I was ready to leave everything and go! My husband was much more levelheaded, with great logic and with much better patience and discipline as well as sense of time and place—he was very smart and logical. Isaak said, "After you complete your education, then we will go." He was right as always. It was the right decision.

So in 1979 I graduated from medical school, and we had some serious discussions, and preparation started. The whole extended family and our family were planning to apply for emigration under the Helsinki Accords for reunifying families. We had an invitation to emigrate from my cousin in Israel, who himself had emigrated in 1974.

We lived with Isaak's parents, so we were considered one household. Isaak's sister, with her husband and two boys, lived in the same apartment building, but on the fifth floor without an elevator. We lived on the second floor (and the reason and significance of that will be explained later). There was also my brother and his wife and their four-year-old son and his in-laws, who lived in a house in Vinnytsia. And then there were my parents, who still resided in the city of Stryi, Lviv. We all applied for a permission visa on the same invitation from Israel.

That decision had been brewing and ripening for a few years, and it was not an easy one to make. In spite of bad instances and ever-increasing antisemitism, this was our home and the home of our ancestors! There were good things as well—great culture, music, ballet, theater, art, etc. It was not easy to cross all of that out and start over in a new country with a new culture and a new language! In a way, we were not only making the decision for ourselves but also for many generations that came before us, who tried to leave but could not, and for the generations after us to give them a chance to live in freedom!

We've known other people who dealt with the issues of antisemitism in their own way, changing names and nationality in their passports and continuing to live in the Soviet Union.

I myself was given such a chance in 1970. We had a national census, and the people who collected them went door-to-door and talked to each member of the family eighteen and older. I'd just turned eighteen, and after they were done talking to my parents, they talked to me and asked the usual—name, date of birth, and nationality. When it came to nationality, my reply was simple: "If my mom is Jewish and my dad is Jewish, of course, I am Jewish." Their reply was that it's not necessarily so. You are eighteen and could decide for yourself!

I decided that I could not turn my back on where I come from, and a little seed that my grandfather had planted was growing stronger and stronger. Not only did I not want to turn my back on my faith—I was proud of it!

Going into the big unknown was very scary, but somebody had to do it first!

So, after so many discussions and sleepless nights, we were all ready to apply, essentially at the same time. We had to collect a bunch of different documents to present to the office that made decisions and issued exit visas.

Some of the decisions we made were rather risky and could've backfired. For example, I decided not to start my job. If you had a job when you applied for a visa, you needed to get clearance from many departments. Sometimes the clearances were intentionally withheld, and that would slow down the whole process. So, we decided to just live off Isaak's salary, and I did not report to work.

It was a big gamble. Authorities could've withheld our visa for a year, and then I could've lost my license for not practicing for a year.

Also my whole family was in an uproar saying that if anybody slowed down our emigration process, it would be me, being a new graduate from medical school, breaking the rules and not reporting to work, etc.

We all applied at the end of 1979, and the wait started. It was also a rather difficult time of the Cold War, the Soviet–Afghan War, and the preparation for the 1980 Olympics to be held in Moscow. President Brezhnev held the helm, but barely. He was rather ill.

So, we lived in a two-room newer apartment on the second floor of a five-story building. My in-laws were older and ill. Isaak's father was almost eighty-three and in poor health. Doctors were saying that he would not last three days, and that was how frequently we had an ambulance at our apartment. He had end-stage congestive heart failure. Isaak's mom, Riva, was younger but suffered from severe depression. Our daughter, Lilya, was barely five.

Little did we know, somebody of importance in OVIR, the office that grants exit visas, really liked our apartment, and within four to five months, we were one of the first in the family to receive permission to leave the Soviet Union. As simple as that! We had to get an extension for one month because of my father-in-law's poor health, but we were finally told that we could not postpone anymore and if we didn't go, permission would be withdrawn! Our apartment turned out to be a hot commodity!

So, now we had to go, and we had absolutely no idea how we would be able to do it. Isaak's father was so frail that he could not even walk, and there were no wheelchairs or stretchers. Isaak ended up essentially carrying his father through Europe.

What came next was also an interesting episode in our life. So, when we were granted permission, Isaak decided to work at a factory where he had been in charge of building as a construction engineer, project manager. It was a big commercial building, and it was a factory for polishing diamonds. He wanted to learn the trade so he could do something with his hands and work in the new country, even if he didn't speak the language. The name of the factory was Crystal.

Of course, everyone in management knew him, as he had been in charge of construction. So, he talked to the director of HR, who was very receptive and said that it was just a matter of all small formalities. He asked him to come in the next day with all the necessary documents, and one of those documents was his passport. By the way, in his construction work, Isaak went by Igor, as Isaak was "too Jewish." He returned the next day as agreed, and as the director looked at his passport and saw Isaak's real name, his face color changed, and he profusely apologized and told Isaak that he was "overqualified." He never got the job.

Another setback happened just as we were given permission to leave the Soviet Union—my parents received a denial on their application. I traveled with my parents to Lviv to ask for an explanation for reasons to refuse their plea. The official didn't have one, and without ever taking his eyes off his desk, he pointed to the door and stated that would be all.

My brother and Isaak's sister didn't hear anything, and both of their families had to go through many years of hardship and very difficult time.

As we crossed the border into Czechoslovakia (now Czech Republic) and underwent a very demeaning and humiliating experience at the Russian checkpoint, my heart ached, as I didn't know if I would ever see my parents or my brother again.

It was at the border that I said to myself, "I will never go back." Why? To be humiliated again? I never went back. It's been forty years!

It was April of 1980, and we were on our way to the new WORLD!

7

EMIGRATION

AND THERE WE WERE. FIVE OF US: MYSELF; MY SWEET HUSBAND, ISAAK; OUR five-year-old daughter, Lilya; and my ailing parents-in-law, Riva and Wolf. Wolf was eighty-three years old with congestive heart failure and early stages of dementia, and Riva was younger at sixty-eight but had depression, anxiety, and congenital heart disease.

We set out for the Big Unknown not even sure how we would get to where we were going, not to mention not knowing the language, the culture, or anything about the country we were going to. Quick reminder that we were leaving from behind the Iron Curtain and way before Google and cell phones, so the information was just not available—or the little that we read in a newspaper was always painted in dark colors of propaganda or caricatures of fat Americans with extremely impolite gestures like putting their legs on the table. That was our view of the country that we were going to.

Also finances. There we were with five people we were responsible for, and we had no idea how we would get from point A to point B. How would we pay for train passes, airplane tickets, and living expenses? At that time the rules in the Soviet Union were such that no matter what you had in your possession or how long you'd worked to accumulate some savings, you were only allowed to exchange $90 per adult person (over eighteen). So, our family of three had $180 in our pockets. Isaak's parents had $180 for them. Baggage was limited to one container per family, which we filled with basic household goods—a couple of rugs, pillows, blankets, pots and pans, dishes, etc. Then we could have just one suitcase per person to bring with us, which we literally had to carry through the whole of Europe. Isaak and I each had to carry two suitcases, as my in-laws were simply not capable of carrying their own, and then we had two items that in the last week before departure we realized needed to be approved by the Ministry of Culture in Moscow as a national treasures and we would have to carry them with us through all checkpoints. One included three or four albums of Isaak's stamp collection, which were rather heavy and sealed with that hot brown seal and in brown paper with rather uncomfortable string around it. The other was a wood carved deer head with antlers. I am still not sure how either of those were national treasures. (My daughter-in-law almost put them in a Goodwill pile the other day.) And yet another thing that we carried through Europe and even forty years later was something my grandma told me to buy, though I don't understand why, as no one plays it. It is an instrument called a bandura, a beautiful Ukrainian national musical instrument, and it is large! It was in a leather case, and we carried it on our shoulders through Europe.

So there we were with a child, ailing parents, and seven or eight pieces of luggage on a train to Chop, a border city in Ukraine, where we were going to go through the final checkpoint and be on another train to Czechoslovakia. My brother, Naum, traveled with us, just to see us out of the country. In Chop we went through a rather unpleasant and humiliating screening by a Ukrainian guard. It was unpleasant enough that I decided there and then, "I will never come back if I get out!!!!" Some stuff was confiscated as "contraband," such as silver-plated cufflinks in one of Isaak's shirts that he had folded and forgotten about. Not only were they taken, but we also had to pay a fine, and it was good that my brother was there waiting on the other side of the fence while we went through the screening. He had to pay the fine for us, as we didn't have any rubles. Isaak's ring was also confiscated as it had a "microchip" of diamond and wasn't allowed. That was Isaak's engagement ring! My daughter's earrings were taken off her five-year-old ears and scrutinized under the microscope, scraped, as they thought that we were hiding diamonds in those emerald earrings! They did return them, and I put them back in my daughter's ears.

Then we were on a train to Prague. In Prague just a quick change of train, and we were on the way to Vienna! We had to get help with luggage and pay for it or we would miss our connection. Anyway, even with all the chaos and fear, we were on the other side of the Iron Curtain!

Before I go on with my story, I would like to acknowledge the incredible agency by the name of HIAS (Hebrew Immigrant Aid Society), which helped us with everything through our journey! I am endlessly grateful and a lifelong supporter of this agency. They were the people who provided both physical and financial assistance on our difficult journey, including train and plane tickets, daily living arrangements, and information on where to go and what to do, and so on.

So, we arrived by train to this beautiful, all in bright lights (it was evening), Vienna. A car took us to our apartment. We looked through the windows in complete awe! Everything was so glamorous. The storefronts full of goods looked very unaffordable for us!!! My father-in-law, in his dementia, watched from the front seat of the car and said, "Vinnytsia"—the city we'd left from in Ukraine—"is really beautiful and bright tonight." We smiled and told him that we liked it too! We were supposed to spend two or three days in Vienna, and then after an interview and all needed paperwork was processed, we'd move on to Italy for further processing and emigration clearance.

At that time, as we learned from other refugees, people stayed in Italy for their clearance for one to two months, which we called "Roman holiday" or *Rimskiye kaniculi* in Russian. The next morning we were picked up and taken to the office for the interview, and the intake worker kept asking questions via an interpreter and glancing at my father-in-law, Wolf, who was visibly dyspneic (short of breath). Then after the short interview, she told us that Wolf couldn't go on the train from Vienna to Rome, as he would not make it! She added: "He would die on the train." She suggested that he needed to be admitted to the hospital and treated. We agreed, and he was taken to the hospital straight from the office. He, of course, was admitted, and the hospital was on the other side of town. We walked there daily, as we could not afford the local bus or train transportation, and taxi fares were out of the question. But we were young and walking was not an issue; plus, we realized, when we crossed town, we could see more.

That is how one day we literally stumbled upon a beautiful mansion, and it was Schönbrunn Palace. We could not dream of seeing it inside, but we saw it from the outside and walked in a beautiful garden. Maybe someday I could go back and see it inside, I dreamed. So in the ten days that Wolf was in the hospital and we went to visit him daily, I remember seeing Vienna really well on our walking expeditions. Also our apartment where we stayed those ten days was across the street from the opera house, and every evening I would come out to see people coming for the performance. Those gorgeous ladies in long dresses and handsome men in tuxedos! Just BEAUTIFUL! So, in those ten days we walked and saw a lot, and we even learned how to buy some food by going to the stores and a farmers market.

We tasted some food that we had never tried before, and some tasted so good (yogurt, for example) that forty years later, I still remember the taste! Same with bananas—I had only had a very green banana in Russia twice in my thirty years. When I went to the farmers market to buy two bananas, I wasn't sure what language they would speak and when I listened, I decided to try my little knowledge of Yiddish, and it worked. I bought two bananas, one for our daughter and one for my in-laws. Isaak and I tasted one bite each from our daughter's banana, and I still remember that taste! The best thing that I ever tasted!

Finally after ten days of treatment, my father-in-law returned to our apartment, and the next morning we were scheduled to take the train to Rome. When morning came and we had to go, Wolf said, "I like it here, and I am not going anywhere." When the car came and we loaded the luggage, we went back and got my father-in-law on each side, essentially carrying him to the car. A wheelchair would've been nice to have, but we didn't know anything about them and obviously did not know to ask for one.

We arrived in Rome, were met by the volunteers from HIAS, who took us to our apartment and gave us a weekly allowance to live on. In the morning we walked to the office and went through an interview where they told us that after three days in Rome being "processed," we needed to find a place to live either in Ostia or Ladispoli (small suburbs outside the Rome metropolitan area, about a forty-minute train ride from the center). We probably would stay there for one month.

In Rome we met another family of four from our town, and the next day the head of their family and Isaak were on a train to Ladispoli to find an apartment. This family was on their way to New York to join their daughter. The parents were older than us, and the wife's parents were a little older than Wolf. We got a room in Ladispoli all together. We stretched a few sheets across the room, and each family had half of the room—four of them on one side of the room and five of us on the other side of the room—with a communal kitchen on the same floor.

To supplement our allowance, Isaak worked in a warehouse close by. He unloaded boxes of wine, and besides small pay he would also bring home a good Italian bread daily and a bottle of wine once a week. Still the only thing that we could afford was pasta, bread, and turkey wings (toward the end of the month, we could not stand them, and we called them "Soviet, Communist wings," or *Krilya Sovetov*). We survived and even managed to see places like Florence, Pisa, and Venice.

After about two weeks in Italy, Isaak told me that he had blood in his urine and then developed fullness and pain in his right testicle. Kidney stone. Strain from lifting heavy boxes???? Then he saw a doctor, who did a biopsy and told him that he had varicocele. He was still uncomfortable but went on with his daily routine and work. Then all three of us were away to Rome for a few days and asked our roommates to keep an eye on our parents. When we returned, we learned that Isaak's mom, Riva, went fully dressed and with her watch into the ocean and probably would've drowned if not for Gregory (our roommate), who pulled her out of the ocean. That was her breakdown episode. Forgot to tell you that since before we left, I had been giving her injections that were prescribed for her severe depression. She really lost it before we left, as she learned that she would have to leave her furniture behind as we left Russia! In spite of all of that, we were planning to also go and see Capri and Pompeii, but it did not happen. Years later we did, and it cost us much more, but we did it. We closed the Italian emigration chapter!

Now we were finally on a plane to New York, arriving June 3, 1980. Our first step on American soil was in New York. As we were talking to the people who met us from the agency, my in-laws decided to go ahead. They had never been on an escalator before, and by the time we reached the escalator we could see that Riva was on the floor at the bottom, as she probably did not know how to step off the escalator and Wolf, who ran to rescue her, was lying on the top of the escalator. The escalator was stopped. We collected both of them, and luckily there were no broken bones! We were dropped off at the hotel and settled into two rooms (what a luxury!!!!) on the same floor.

The next morning we would depart for Portland, Oregon, where my grandma and two cousins were awaiting us! Just as we got to our room after assuring that my in-laws were okay, our daughter, Lilya, announced that she urgently needed to go to the bathroom for number two. We looked in the bathroom and were sure the toilet was "broken." You see, in Russia there was never a water level in a toilet bowl. You flush and the water goes down, but none comes up back. So, naturally when we saw the water level in a toilet bowl, we presumed that it was broken! I know—who would think of it now? So, we rushed to my in-laws' room, and their toilet was broken too! Our daughter was desperate now, so we let her go, and the story has a happy ending, as you can imagine. The cultural lessons from step one!

The next morning after briefly being put on and taken off from a plane to Portland, Maine (as we found out later), we were finally on our way to Denver, Colorado, where we would be connecting to Portland, Oregon.

As we arrived to Denver, we weren't met by anyone from the agency. What happened? But I was looking at my tickets and had absolutely not even the slightest idea what I was looking at? Mute and deaf! No way to ask anybody for help! No idea what gate we needed or even the flight number. My anxiety was so high. What to do? It probably was all written and stamped on my face, as this nice "true cowboy" type approached me and asked if he could help. An American cowboy would help me? Remember that I'd only seen some bad caricatures of them, and deeply rooted negative propaganda was engraved into my subconscious!? I was very desperate, though, and I handed him our tickets. He took one look, went to the nearest intercom system on a wall, and told them something. A few minutes later a shuttle that looked like a stretched golf cart arrived (I had never seen one before). The cowboy talked to the driver and then motioned to my in-laws to get on it. They did. Then he looked at the tickets again and motioned for us to get on with all the luggage. He talked to the driver again, and we took off on a joyride. We were going fast. As we stopped, the driver pointed toward the entrance of the plane and said, "Go, go!"

We were on the plane, and even before we put our seat belts on, the engine started. We would most definitely have missed that flight if not for THAT cowboy! I'll remember him FOREVER!

We were flying, and they were bringing food and drinks. We were hungry and thirsty and dying to try Coca-Cola, but we politely declined, waving no, as we did not know that food and drinks were a part of your ticket, and we were afraid that we would have to pay for it! We definitely did not know the word *complimentary*! But that was not important! Just another one of many cultural lessons! What was important is that we were finally on our way to our new home in Portland, Oregon!

8

ARRIVING AT OUR NEW HOME!
COMING TO AMERICA!

AFTER YEARS OF ALL THOSE MIXED EMOTIONS (APPREHENSION, INDECI-siveness, doubts, fear of the unknown, anxiety, curiosity, and even occasionally very guarded excitement), we were finally leaving the USSR and heading for the border and to the USA!!!

Everything was new and exciting but also scary as we were going into the unknown!!!! Did we make the right decision? My husband and I were both in our thirties, both professionals, but we didn't have the language or knowledge of the culture and country that we were heading to. Our five-and-a-half-year-old daughter, we were responsible for that child! Was it the right decision for her? Also with us were my parents-in-law, both elderly and in frail states of health...

Anyway, April 17, 1980, we were all on the train heading for the border! Skipping unpleasant details of the emigration check point (as it could be alone a separate chapter), we were finally outside the Iron Curtain!!!!! Our train was now chugging into that unknown world, which unfortunately had been colored as "bad" in Russian News. After all it was the time of the Cold War, and information wasn't freely available.

We traveled for a month and a half through Vienna, Austria, and then Italy (which was a big shock, as we had never been out of the country!). We received news that on June 2, 1980, we would board a plane for New York and then connect to Portland, Oregon, via Denver (as it turned out). After briefly being loaded on a plane for Portland, Maine, we were taken off, and finally we were all on a plane for Portland, Oregon.

Just to backtrack for a minute, our only contact in Portland was my seventy-eight-year-old grandma, who'd left Ukraine with my cousin, her grandson. He was a single young man who worked a lot and was too busy to write! Grandma, who'd emigrated just two years ago at the age of seventy-six had been writing to us, and her letters were rather very descriptive. She would say that Portland is rainy but very clean and green and a beautiful city! And she added: "You are going to love it!" She also talked in her letters about the Rose Festival, even though she only saw it on TV once and loved it!

We were finally arriving at the Portland airport on June 4, 1980, and were picked up by agency representatives (none of them, of course, spoke any Russian and we did not speak English). We'd just spent six weeks in Europe without newspapers, news, or TV? We were absolutely ignorant and, in a way, mute and deaf!

As we were driving toward the city, we eagerly took in the sights. As we crossed beautiful bridges, we looked out the windows on both sides with our daughter sitting in the middle between us.

We saw incredible amount of dirt everywhere—covering sidewalks, cars, houses! After some time, we looked at each other, and I said, "Clean city???? What clean city?" Adding: "Grandma completely lost her marbles!!!!!"

I did mention that we arrived in Portland on June 4, 1980, merely two weeks after Mount Saint Helens erupted on May 19, 1980, but we didn't know that then. It took two months for us to learn about Mount Saint Helens, and that was by pure chance.

Still not understanding why the city was so filthy, we were placed in an apartment on 5th Avenue in town. We heard about the Rose Festival and were given a map by one of the volunteers, so we headed there one week after we arrived. The first week was very busy with trying to settle in (unpacking pots and pans and brooms brought by those nice volunteers), some health issues, etc. At this point we pretty much accepted the fact that we lived in the dirtiest place in America!

So, we were on our way to the parade, which was a few blocks from our apartment. Isaak, my husband, was looking on the map given to us by the volunteer. I was looking at people and immediately noticed that half of the people were wearing masks and the other half were smiling and greeting us!!!

You see, in Russia, the only people who wear masks are people with tuberculosis, as they are contagious! And smiling and greeting strangers on the street is at the least impolite but often was a sign of mental instability! It's a cultural thing, but you just do not smile and greet strangers! That was engraved in our subconscious.

I turned to my husband and said: "Not only did we come to the dirtiest place on earth, but half of the people have tuberculosis and are contagious and the other half are plain crazy!!!!"

We never made it to the first Rose Festival parade, as it was difficult to breathe (but we were not sure why). Then it was plain scary to walk among so many people with TB and mental instability!

As I mentioned previously, two months later we learned about Mount Saint Helen's volcanic eruption, and then all of the pieces of the puzzle fell into place. We learned about the volcanic ash and mask use, and about just being friendly when greeting someone in the street.

There were, of course, other cultural lessons later on, but looking back on this one always brings out that warm smile.

When I was in Japan (and everybody there wears a mask), I asked people on the street and in the subway as to why they do that. I received many different explanations, but I thought of my "mask story" and smiled again!

And now, when I walk in the street and greet and smile at complete strangers, it always warms my heart to do it! It feels wonderful! This world needs more kindness, smiles, and hugs. After all, we are all citizens of this world, Planet Earth, and even though languages and distances and cultures separate us, love, kindness, and smiles bring us together!

Let's smile more and hate less, and hopefully world peace will embrace this beautiful planet with a smile!!!!

9

DIFFICULT BEGINNINGS— LAUGHTER AND TEARS

I RODE ON THE BUS APPROACHING MY BUS STOP ON MY FIRST RIDE HOME from college classes, and I could see that the bus wasn't planning to stop. You see, everywhere in Europe and the Soviet Union, the buses stop at each assigned stop regardless of whether anybody gets off or on the bus. Expecting the same and hearing a strange buzzing intermittently, I missed my stop. The buzzing was, of course, people requesting a stop, but I was standing and did not see people pressing the yellow strip on the side of the bus (I know it now!). In a panic I made my way to the driver almost shouting: "Stop, please stop!" He looked very strangely at me and of course stopped at the next stop! Looking back at that, I know how ridiculous it looked, but I wasn't laughing then, walking one stop back on the very busy Beaverton-Hillsdale Highway. At that time, it did not even have a white strip separating the walkers from the cars going by. Scary experience!

Another cultural lesson came when our six-year-old daughter came home from preschool and asked me: "Mommy, what is a Commie?" I asked why and she replied, "That is what all the kids call me in school!" That was the time of the Cold War. I had someone running away from me on a bus stop just because she asked where I was from, and I told her that I was from the USSR! Fear is an incredibly powerful emotion and especially if it is government sponsored and created! How do you explain that to a six-year-old?

Then came a very serious cultural lesson, which we did not even understand at the time. Our daughter started her swimming classes at the Jewish community center. We signed her up, and a school bus would drop her off after school for the lessons. Isaak and I were both in school learning English at Portland Community College (PCC) at that time and never had the chance to see her class and group. She went two or three times, and then when we would pick her up and walk home after class, she would cry and say, "That it is not how everybody else is dressed..." We had no clue what she was talking about. She said that she was not going back, and she cried all the time. Finally I took an excuse from my classes and went to her swimming class. You see, in Russia at that time, it was standard for girls to wear just colorful underwear and no top almost until puberty. When I came to class, I saw even smaller children wearing full swimsuits while Lilya had just her underwear. I understood why my daughter was crying and refusing to go to the swimming classes.

That afternoon I went to the agency and discussed the issue with them and told them that I was just not able to afford $10 for a swimsuit. We mostly bought our clothes used at Goodwill, but a swimsuit for a child was too personal for that. The social worker's facial expression was disbelief, anger, and surprise. She gave me a check for $10, and Lilya and I walked directly to the Newberry's store in downtown Portland to buy her a swimming suit. I was so thrilled to be able to do it and for our daughter to continue her swimming classes. She became very good at it and eventually joined a swim team.

And then we received devastating news maybe three or four weeks after arrival! Remember that Isaak had started seeing blood in his urine and having testicular pain while we were in Italy? Isaak was diagnosed with testicular cancer at age thirty.

I was so heartbroken, crying day and night. Grandma was the only person there to console me. We did not even speak English, and here was this horrible news, and Isaak needed two major surgeries! You see, in Russia the mentality was that a diagnosis of any kind of cancer was a death sentence. Frequently medical professionals would not tell the patient about their fatal disease—like in Isaak's case, how he was told that he had a varicocele or urinary tract infection. The logic behind it was why let somebody know that they are dying and rob them of the short time they have left to enjoy life? It was a common medical practice in Russia. Family would be informed of the diagnosis and usually the poor prognosis, but not the patient. When I suggested the same tactic for Isaak, the urologist told me that he could not do it and informed Isaak of his diagnosis and the need for two major surgeries! So, together we lived through that horrible time.

A month later Isaak had had his surgeries and recovered and had started his evening job as a dishwasher at the West Hills Village retirement facility. In the mornings he took English and later computer classes and eventually became a computer programmer. I did some interpretation work and also got a job as a companion for older patients. I'm very proud to say that as difficult as those times were, we struggled through them together and never received a single welfare check!

That time had a lot of tears and occasional laughter and numerous cultural lessons, but we were young with great desire to succeed and make a better life for ourselves and our children.

Laughter was always a big part of life, so I want to conclude this chapter with another cultural "funny" story, which was not in the least funny at that time! Isaak went to Western Business College to get his computer education, and they accepted some of his credentials from his engineering degree, but he still had to take an admission test. So he went to the college campus in downtown Portland and was taken to the room for the test. He was given a paper and a pencil and was advised on the time window to complete the answers and left alone in the room. As he described later, the room was very, very hot, but he thought that maybe he was being tested in a certain climatic condition intentionally, as the work with computers might require that.

So here Isaak was sweating his brain out while concentrating on questions and completing the test. At the end, the instructor came back to the room and said that he was really sorry for the room being so very hot, as something was wrong with the thermostat—it was as simple as that...Isaak passed the test and was admitted to that college.

But the mentality of being tested in the heat or other cultural discrepancies that we survived was a big part of who we were and what kind of determination we needed to survive and to succeed as we were going into the unknown. Failure was not an option!

Frequently we would be asked if we were missing our "home," and we would always reply, "We are HOME!" By the way, when we left the Soviet Union, we were stripped of our citizenship, had to give up our passports, and were required to pay authorities 700 rubles (about three to four months' salary at the time) for that. Russia was frequently called Mother Russia, but as one *refusenik* Anatoly Shcharansky explained, if a mother treats me like that, I would rather be an orphan! For five years, we were stateless until we were allowed to take the naturalization test and become citizens of the USA.

Yes, even though almost my whole family (parents, brother with his family, and Isaak's sister and her family) was still in Ukraine and we were not sure if we would ever see them again, the mindset was: "Yes, we left the country for good. There is no going back, and this is our home, and we need to make the best of it we can, even in impossible circumstances." As I said, no going back. We threw away the key and burned the bridges.

We of course missed our family, but we never felt nostalgia or homesickness. This was our new home, and we were determined to succeed!

10

FIRST STEPS ARE ALWAYS TOUGH

WE WERE IN OUR NEW COUNTRY, NEW CULTURE, NEW LANGUAGE AND START-ing our new life!!! All our experiences were new, and we were here in our new home to make it work for us and the generations to come! And as the saying goes, the first steps are always hard.

Isaak was recovering from two major surgeries. What a trauma right upon arrival, and what a difficult experience it was! Now, I can smile sometimes looking back on that. Some of it was ridiculous and funny, and it always came with another cultural lesson. Isaak accepted the unwelcome news very bravely, ready to fight.

My memory of meeting his surgeon brings out a smile, though. You see, in Russia in medical school, I studied the Latin language, and we were all told that Latin is an international medical language. If you speak Latin, you could speak to any doctor in the world! Isaak's surgeon at St. Vincent's hospital preferred to meet at 5:00 a.m., and when we met and I started to talk to him in Latin, he looked at me like I was from another planet. Then he asked me to have an interpreter next time. I had been trying to avoid asking for an interpreter and had sat frequently until after midnight with the dictionary to translate every word for the questions I wanted to ask. I made a list and was ready to read it to the surgeon at 5:00 a.m. A few times for other appointments, my cousin Stan had been able to come and help to interpret, but he worked full-time and was in the country for two years. After my initial appointment with the surgeon, I realized very quickly that Latin is not an international medical language!

So Isaak had his major surgeries, and the second one lasted seven and a half hours for exploratory abdominal surgery. Then he was cleared and told it had not spread to lymph nodes or other organs—he was determined to be cancer-free and with no further treatment needed! First major VICTORY after a major fight. Right after the surgery, talking through the interpreter, we were told that we probably would not be able to have any more children. At that time, that was the last thing that we were thinking about. I just had my seventy-eight-year-old grandma's shoulder to cry on. My parents had been refused their exit visa, and I didn't know if I would ever see them again. The surgeon told us that he had one daughter about our daughter's age and he was happy with one child. Our daughter was almost six.

That brings me to another "funny" story. Believe me again that it was not funny at the time. So, our daughter was turning six at the end of August. We had been in the country a little over two months. Not speaking the language yet, Isaak was recovering from surgeries and on a very limited income. We were always grateful for what we had, but simply put, we were very poor. But it was our daughter's first birthday in her new home, new country. In the apartment where we lived, there were maybe three or four kids her age, and she had two cousins a little older. So, we invited five to six kids! What to do? What to prepare? Being very frugal, I decided on making *vareniki* (which is a ravioli-like dish that is common in Ukraine). Usually it's a dough stuffed with meet or cottage cheese or potato. On a budget, I went and picked blackberries from the bushes nearby and decided to make fruit ravioli to surprise the kids. It did not go well, as berries mixed with sugar were very juicy, and it was hard to keep the raviolis closed with that. I added more flour, and after a rather labor-intensive day, I managed to salvage some and put them on a serving plate. Vareniki are usually eaten with sour cream. Some of the kids were from Russian-speaking families who'd arrived before us; others were not, but they did not touch my creation and their eyes where saying, "What is that?" My grandma baked a pound cake, and that saved the day! Little did I know then that after the kids played in the courtyard, they expected a pizza, hamburgers, or at least hot dogs and a cake. Not only did we not know that, but we could not dream of affording such luxuries.

It sure was an interesting birthday for our daughter! We had many more down the road at McDonald's, Burger King, Chuck E. Cheese, water parks, and bumper cars, but that first one here was a complete fiasco and another cultural lesson!

We slowly started taking steps toward independence with jobs and schools, as our federal support was coming to an end. We were grateful that it helped us in those initial steps while we were learning how to speak. Isaak was told to check with welfare, as he potentially may qualify for assistance following those surgeries. He went to apply once and then came home and said that he couldn't consider accepting welfare. "What can I do?" he asked. "I have ten years of engineering in Ukraine but no language here!"

Then we were at this one dinner that someone had invited us to, and the surgeon who'd recently operated on Isaak was volunteering and appeared to be very familiar with carrying those plates. When we asked, he said that that was how he'd put himself through medical school. At that point Isaak knew that he could do any job! The titles, subordination, experience did not matter anymore. Isaak was very happy to get his first job on a swing shift as a dishwasher at a local retirement facility. That allowed him to attend classes in the morning at Western Business College, where he began to learn computer science.

We also had an English tutor volunteer with us two times a week. Her name was Alice Metcalf, a retired high school English teacher. She was the loveliest, sweetest lady and tried to incorporate real-life events and sports in teaching us English. She was teaching the culture! I'm not sure if she loved baseball or just chose it as a part of the overall cultural experience, but she repeatedly tried to explain it to us but to no avail. It was a new sport to us. We knew basketball, soccer, volleyball, gymnastics, swimming, figure skating, skiing, and chess well both as a participants in high school and as spectators but not baseball! That sweet Alice spent hours explaining innings, bases, and home runs, but we just could not get it. And in frustration she would say that she didn't understand how two intelligent people could not understand such a simple and popular game. Another cultural lesson!

Just jumping a little bit ahead years later to when we went to Chicago for the first time to see our daughter and meet her significant other, Chad. He was excited and announced that he had tickets to see the Cubs play, and we had to politely decline, as it would've been pointless. Jumping a little bit ahead even more in my story, after watching two generations play and my grandkids umpire for a little league, I finally thought, *I've got it!!!* At one game my grandkids were playing, the parents chanted, "Gooday gooday." I asked my daughter what they were saying or what kind of call that was. She replied that they were saying, "Good eye, good eye," and I am saying it now too and even appropriately so. Since then I've watched a few Seattle Mariners games and even began to enjoy it, but once in a while I need to clarify some details with my grandson. I guess baseball is just something you need to grow up with!

Back to the eighties—Isaak was working as a dishwasher at the retirement home. Isaak always took pride in every job he had. So he came home and told me how proud he was to complete a rather busy shift and do the best job that he could. Then one day he told me that there was one nurse who was very tall and always came to work in high heels and was very friendly to him. Isaak was five-foot-ten, and he told me that the nurse was at least a head taller. We later learned that that nurse was a transvestite, and it was a completely foreign concept to us. I am not saying that there were no transgender people in the USSR, but the concept was deeply closeted and a taboo to talk about it. Another cultural lesson. And we learned more as we walked through our new life. Life was busy, complicated often, but we learned and remained determined to succeed!

We continued to study English and also learned how to live on a very limited income from a dishwasher's job (luckily we both were frugal). We were young, able to learn, learning to adjust, and we were happy!

A few months later, I became rather ill with nausea, vomiting, and fatigue. Maybe flu or food poisoning, I thought, but after a month of symptoms, I found out that I was pregnant! Happiness, confusion, fear, joy? All of the above. Unplanned?

After we had been told that we probably wouldn't be able to have any more children, deep down I badly wanted one. You know that saying that forbidden fruit is always sweet! But I'd been planning on going back to school to try to get my medical credentials. I realized that dream had to be put on hold for now as another dream took priority! So then we were looking forward to welcoming another child in our life! More than ever determined to succeed!

11

BIRTH OF A MIRACLE CHILD

I WAS VERY HAPPY TO BE PREGNANT AGAIN! I WANTED THIS CHILD WITH ALL my soul and all my might! Besides Isaak, my only support was my seventy-nine-year-old grandmother. She was very strong, wiping away my tears and alleviating my fears. Time was flying, and there I was six months pregnant. I appeared "very pregnant," as grandma was accommodating my unstoppable craving for strawberries a little too well. Because it wasn't just strawberries. I craved vareniki (remember those ravioli-like things) but with strawberries inside. I had a little too many of those!!!

Good news arrived from Ukraine. After having received a refusal to leave the Soviet Union at the time of our departure, suddenly my sweet parents, Anna and Mikhail Chernobelsky, were given permission and an exit visa from Ukraine. One month later we were reunited in Portland. Tears of happiness upon their arrival. They came very close to my baby due date. How great for me. By the way, I had no ultrasounds, so I did not know whether I was having a boy or a girl, but it did not matter. All that mattered was that the baby was healthy!

My parents had never studied English, so my mom was eager to start classes. We were talking about them starting English as a Second Language (ESL) classes at PCC, and my mom got excited, but my dad pointed to my very sizable pregnant abdomen and simply said: "My studies and my job are right there!" That is how I was very lucky to get the best babysitters in the world and at a very reasonable price (free!!!).

Time flew by really fast. Right upon arrival, my mom ended up in the hospital for emergency gallbladder removal surgery, which was complicated by a post-op infection! Anyway, June came along, and while I was in class at the PCC Sylvania campus on June 4, 1981 (our one-year anniversary of arriving in Portland), I felt that I needed to go home. By the way, I was so big that I would not fit in a desk. I sat sideways, which was very uncomfortable, and there I was having contractions. My instructor was so terrified, and he said for me to leave immediately and that I passed all the classes with good grades, etc. One difficulty was that I had commuted by bus—we did not have a car for our first two years in America. What to do? Isaak was downtown, and he got there by bus. My cousin was at work. One very nice assistant instructor in the class was the loveliest lady (who gave me all her maternity clothes) and volunteered to take me home.

I came home and was resting. Isaak came home from his classes. My pain somewhat resolved, and we decided to wait at home. I did not sleep much, as I was very uncomfortable. As I mentioned, there had been no ultrasound, but when I looked at my abdomen, it looked VERY asymmetrical. I told my OBGYN, Dr. Lawson, about it, and I suspected that the baby was in an abnormal position. He said that everything was okay.

So very early on June 5, we were going to Good Sam very early in the morning. My doctor was on vacation, and a different doctor came to deliver. When he examined me, he said that the asymmetry that I was referring to was my baby's legs in the upper-left corner of my abdomen and even though the baby's head was down, the baby was in a diagonal position. For a while, the doctor tried a manual external rotation, but it did not work, and then around eight p.m., he said that the baby was tired, took big forceps, and delivered a big and tired boy at 8:15 p.m. His weight was 10.2 pounds, and he was 22.5 inches long. His nickname was BIG BOY! My doctor asked, "Who is so big in the family?" and I replied, "Grandma." My grandma was by my side all the time, as Isaak had turned white and was about to faint and the doctor asked him to sit down on the side. Grandma was holding my hand and kept saying that I could pull her beautiful white hair when I was in pain if that would help me. Yes, my grandma was holding my hand and reassuring me all the way through labor and saw David's birth. Sixteen years later she passed away in her sleep on June 5, 1997.

We named our son David, for the doctor who'd operated on Isaak and saved his life! The breastfeeding went much better the second time around, and David was completely breast fed until he was eleven month old! And of course another funny story...

Eight days after David's birth, we were preparing for Bris (or Brit) milah, ritual Jewish circumcision. We were at the hospital room preparing for that. Dr. David would be performing the procedure, so he set up all his needed instruments at the table. Our daughter, who was almost seven at the time, saw all the preparation and began to cry bitterly. What happened? She was extremely scared and told us that she wanted a little brother and was afraid that after they did what they were going to do, she would have a sister instead. She was inconsolable! We reassured her that she would always be a big sister to her little brother and nothing would change. It was a beautiful ceremony, and between my mom and grandma, the production of yummy, yummy baked goods were unbelievable! Everybody left with a lunch bag full of treats!

Our miracle, unexpected child with blue eyes and blond hair was a gift from above! As I said above, when David turned eleven months old and I was lucky to have great—the best possible— babysitters, I started looking into options on how to get my medical credentials back in America. The agency that helped us with resettlement had never had a doctor before me, so they did not know how to start the process. I started going to the library to look through medical books, just to see what I could understand or not. One day I went to the library at Oregon Health & Science University (OHSU). I was standing in a medical books aisle and looking through the books. A few feet from me, I saw a very distinguished-looking gray-haired gentlemen with glasses looking at similar books. We started talking, both with heavy accents, but we seemed to understand each other. The man was an ophthalmologist from Nicaragua, and his name was Ernesto Garay! He was the one who gave me all the information and address in Philadelphia for me to inquire about the process and request an application and requirements for the test. After my inquiry, I sent them my diploma, but I had a really hard time explaining why my diploma was a typed-up document with a brown seal rather than a photocopy of the document. It was almost impossible for the office to understand that photocopies did not exist in Russia at that time.

Now our son, David, was one and our daughter, Lilya, was eight, and I was starting my preparations toward my medical degree in America. I was applying to Stanley H. Kaplan courses in downtown Portland. Not only did I have to study English in order to pass the TOEFL test and medical and basic science tests to pass the two-day medical part, but I also had to learn how to do multiple-choice tests. As strange as it sounds, I had never previously done multiple-choice questions. In Russia I had sure taken a lot of tests in my seven years in medical school, but they were always in the form of direct questions that we had to write full answers to. At the age of thirty, I had never had a multiple-choice test!!!

At the Kaplan center I studied like I was on a job eight a.m. to five p.m. (thank you to my parents again for allowing me to do that; they completely took care of our two kids). Studying was hard, but it was a wonderful place where I met so many people from different parts of the world! Lunchtime was fun, and we all gathered to talk about our experiences, share our studies, and laugh.

One day my administrator asked me to take a picture for my official ID card. I got ready and sat there very seriously. Barbara, the administrator, asked me to smile, but I would not do it. My whole class was behind Barbara making faces and waving their hands, but I would not smile! People who know me now find it hard to believe, as I am always laughing. For thirty years I had been conditioned not to smile on any official document—and the center ID was an official document! Even forty years later I find that it is still hard for me to smile when my picture is taken (like for a passport or the DMV).

After studying for six months (in a course that was designed for a year), I requested an application from Philadelphia for the ECFMG test. When the documents arrived, I realized that the application for the test was $250 or $300, which was an enormous amount of money at the time! Isaak, the sole provider for our family of four, had just started his first computer tech job, which paid better than his dishwasher job but still very modestly. Also, the test was given only twice a year, and the closest places that I could take the test were Seattle or Olympia, Washington. The test was two full days, which meant at least two nights in a hotel. It was all very expensive, but I decided that I needed to try to see what the test was all about and how I would do on a clock with multiple choices. I was not quite ready, but I needed to try. We went to Olympia for the first time. After just two or three years in the country, I took this very difficult test, and four to six weeks after the test, my results were not surprisingly low (69 or 70—a 75 was required to pass).

The next test would be given in Seattle, and after six more months of studying, I felt really good and sure that I had passed the test that time. Very confident, but still anxious, I awaited the results, and six weeks later I was so excited to open the envelope. But instead of the score, there was a statement. A leak of test material had been discovered in a Caribbean medical school, and therefore ALL test results were canceled. No refund for the application fee, and I had to wait another six months to apply again. I took the test again in 1983 and received a passing score of 79 percent! Elated!

But now to search for a residency. In Portland, impossible. Many programs openly told me not to even apply. But after submitting hundreds and hundreds of applications all over the USA and being almost ready to relocate to New York or Philadelphia (with a long entourage of relatives who depended on me for almost everything), a miracle happened and I was accepted to OHSU in Portland for my public health and preventive medicine residency from 1984 to 1987. In 1988 I passed my FLEX exam (equivalent to the National Board of Medical Examiners) and became a medical doctor in the USA!

12

NEW LIFE AND TERRIBLE NEWS FROM THE SOVIET UNION

OUR LIFE SEEMED TO BE TAKING TURNS IN THE RIGHT DIRECTION. ALL OUR hard work was paying off. Isaak's health was good, and the fear of cancer was somewhat behind us. Isaak was now again being a dreamer. But this time it was not just a dream—he was determined to turn his dream into reality.

Before I tell you what I mean, I need to tell you that Isaak's profession was as a construction engineer/architect—that was his true love. When we came to the USA in 1980, the construction business was essentially nonexistent, so he had to retrain and become a computer programmer, as he was good with logic and numbers! Construction and architecture were definitely Isaak's passion. I never understood it and honestly never had a passion for it!

Whenever Isaak was in the midst of construction, he would desperately tried to explain to me what room the wooden poles would create, and of course, he had a vision, but I did not have a clue. That scenario would repeat through our lives at least twice, and when I looked in his sparkling beautiful eyes full of absolute excitement, passion, and love for what he did, that was where and when I completely fell in love with that wonderful man and his passionate heart. In the future we visited every Street of Dream, and I saw that excitement and spark in his eyes when he looked at some new features and liked them!

So hopefully I've given you a sense that even though Isaak became a very good computer programmer for the next thirty years, his first love remained construction and architecture. In his free time, he would always draw houses and other buildings. He dreamed with a piece of paper and a pencil. He loved looking at blueprints and giving all sorts of advice to people who asked.

At that time we lived in an apartment on 30th Street in the Southwest Portland. It was a great location for a Jewish family to settle, as it was conveniently located close to a public school, a day preschool, and the Jewish community center for after-school activities (e.g., gymnastics, soccer, swimming, and basketball). As a matter of fact, that is where our daughter, Lilya, started and excelled in gymnastics, and because of her competition schedule, we got to explore other places in Oregon like Salem, Woodburn, Eugene, and the Oregon coast for the first time. In Portland we had to choose places for the kids either in walking distance or in proximity to public transportation, as Isaak was the only driver in the family. So my father would take our daughter to and from the school bus. David walked to preschool at Neveh Shalom Foundation School and then up the hill to different after-school activities. I cannot ever adequately express my gratitude for the luxury of having parents who were able and willing to do what mine did for us and our children. My dad didn't drive, and they lived two bus stops away from our apartment, but like a clock, he would take a bus and be at our doorstep at 7:30 a.m. to take care of the kids as we had to leave. Writing about it brings a smile to my face, as every morning he would show up in his suit with a dress shirt and tie like he used to wear for work. And the way he did it with all his love and dedication—that was the best job he did!

Just a little jump to the future—I met a lady at a Friday-night service at the Neveh Shalom synagogue. She came up to me and said that I probably did not remember who she was, and I did not. It turns out that she had been a teacher at the preschool were my dad had taken David every morning for years since he was two years old. She said that she loved seeing my dad so lovingly holding David's hand as they crossed Beaverton-Hillsdale Highway. At the time of that conversation, David was in his thirties, and my dad had passed away when David was eleven, so it had been a long time. I was grateful for the memory.

Back to 1984. I was busy in my residency at OHSU. Isaak had his first real computer job, and my sweet parents watched our kids, and my mom would frequently cook the most delicious dinner for all of us. Life was good! Frequently in the evening we would take walks to Gabriel Park and around the neighborhood to talk about our day. On one of those evening strolls, probably two streets from our apartment, we saw the simple sign: LOT FOR SALE and a phone number. We were not even dreaming about a house yet, but we really got excited about it. Isaak more than me—his vision clicked in, and I was sure that he was starting to draw in his mind. We had only been in the country four years. Isaak was still the sole breadwinner, as my residency was in financial difficulty and I was moonlighting and doing different small jobs to make some money. We'd never owned a house, or even a car for that matter. But almost nobody did in Russia at that time.

So, the next day we called the number and as we were inquiring regarding the price, the owner told us that if we wanted to bargain further, he would not be talking to us! We were confused and told him that it was the first time that we'd called. We did buy that lot and only later found out that a friend of ours was the one who'd bargained and walked away over $1,000. I am sure on the phone we sounded the same with the same accent! A year later we got our first mortgage and line of credit and built our first home! American dream! It goes without saying that Isaak immediately went to the drawing board. He designed a simple split-level home with a woodstove between the living room and bedrooms, and that significantly helped us with our electrical bill! We made it work!

Then at the end of 1985, beginning of 1986, terrible news arrived from Vinnytsia, Ukraine, where my brother and his family remained and had been awaiting permission to leave the Soviet Union for six years by then (remember that we applied altogether?). His wife, Dina, told us that Naum, my brother, had been arrested and jailed on trumped-up charges of forgery and bribery, but it was truly just for his persistent desire to leave the

Soviet Union. I was in a medical office with my father for his appointment when the news arrived. As my father heard that, the stress was too much, and he fainted. He was admitted to the hospital for a heart attack... Our lives were changed with that call.

13

VICTORY AND MY BROTHER'S FAMILY'S ARRIVAL TO PORTLAND!

LIKE MOST OF THE TIME IN LIFE, GOOD AND BAD OFTEN WALK HAND-IN-hand.

With that news, I felt incredible urgency, which I am not even sure I can convey on these pages!!!! I needed to get in touch with Dina (my sister-in-law) to find out more details about what happened and, more importantly, how we could help. How could I do that? They had no phone and very few friends, and neighbors would be afraid to lend their phone, as often the family members of arrested people are closely followed and phone conversations are monitored. It seems like a trivial issue now, and my grandkids' generation will have a hard time even understanding what I am talking about. Stress and fear enveloped us again five years after we thought we'd said goodbye to that FOREVER!

I spent almost a week calling one neighbor and begging her to go see Dina, and I arranged for her to go to their apartment on a certain day and at a certain time at night, where there was a lower chance of being followed and potentially jeopardizing people who were doing us a big favor. After a few very anxious and expensive calls, we are able to convince them, and we called back at the time agreed upon and talked to my sister-in-law, Dina. As much as she was trying to be careful with what she was saying, she did tell us the whole horrible story!

My brother, Naum Chernobelsky, was the only person in the family working at a certain factory. He specialized in refrigeration and air-conditioning systems. Dina had quit her job to make the process of leaving easier (remember, we all applied to leave in 1979), so she had not been working now for six years, and they were living in her childhood home with her mom and my nephew, Mark, nine years old at the time, and my niece, Elana, two years old at the time (she was born in 1983 after our family and my parents had left Ukraine). Dina told me that one day Naum was just arrested at the factory and jailed on trumped-up charges of forgery and bribery but truly just for his persistent desire to leave the Soviet Union and be reunited with his family! Behind closed doors, he was told that if he wanted to emigrate, instead he would go to jail. He was sentenced to eight years in a hard-labor camp. His wife, Dina, and two small kids would be left without any source of income and would have to survive on her mom's very small pension! It was like an emergency light started blinking in my brain instantly: What do I do to help with my brother's fight for his freedom? How can I help the family financially? You see, it was still the time of the Cold War, and Western Union simply did not exist in Russia, so transferring money was not that simple.

Dina, in complete exhaustion, told us that she'd tried everything but frequently "hit the wall." Nobody wanted to take the case because it was politically motivated and financially they were very bad off. Then I asked if she would want us to help her, and she replied, "Yes." Knowing the mentality and the red-tape loopholes of the system, we did not want to make anything worse. From the moment that she said yes, I had absolutely no idea what I could possibly do, but I knew that from that moment on, there was no higher priority for me than saving my brother and his family. THAT FIGHT LITERALLY TOOK OVER MY LIFE!

I probably could write a book about that alone, but in short I left no stone unturned. I contacted every congressman and senator, every dignitary and organization (local and national) that I thought just might help! Sunday school kids wrote numerous letters to Yeltsin and then Gorbachev. I was very fortunate to meet and plead my case to Mr. Elie Wiesel (who happened to be a guest speaker at Linfield College). I learned later that he pled the case of my brother and his family to Gorbachev himself "right at the Red Square in Moscow" (as he later wrote to me). As a child Holocaust survivor, he truly knew the saying that if you save one life, you save all! I spoke on the steps of the Justice Center in downtown Portland as well as at different churches and synagogues. I pled my case to Physicians for Social Responsibility and Doctors without Borders. I picketed with my friends at the

Chkalov Monument, as some dignitaries arrived from Russia to celebrate the anniversary of Chkalov's flight. Isaak and I attended an unforgettable 250,000-person march in Washington, DC, on the Mall with the sign: "Free Naum Chernobelsky." It was an outcry for freedom for so many refusniks (the term used to describe people who were like my brother, denied permission to leave the USSR for no clear reason, and some were imprisoned for no reason whatsoever, like my brother and Natan Sharansky). TV interviews, newspaper interviews, more letters written to Soviet officials over many sleepless nights. Anything and everything that could potentially help.

Now the financial part. As I mentioned, it was not very easy. I was trying to come up with any way to transfer some money to my family in Vinnytsia, Ukraine. So I called my cousin in Israel (his name was also Naum Chernobelsky). He was the one who sent us all invitations and was my father's nephew (but truly like another son, as his father had died in WWII and my father participated in his upbringing after the war). I was discussing with him the horrible predicament that my brother and family were in and how we were desperate to find somebody to transfer some money to the family. He promised to work hard on that, and few days later he found a potential money source. That person's brother lived in Georgia, Russia, and he would be willing to travel by train to Vinnytsia, Ukraine, to deliver money to my family. We would compensate him for his train expenses and of course the money. My cousin would pay the full sum to the person, and we would send cash to my cousin when the deal was completed. We set the whole transaction in motion, but how many sleepless nights would I have before the transaction was done??? You see, my moral compass was telling me that the man in Georgia needed to know about my brother being in jail and my family's desperation, but I worried that if we told him, he probably would not be willing to risk it. You see, when someone was imprisoned, frequently their houses and family members were watched by KGB agents... So, in my sleepless nights I had visions of this nice man being followed and arrested, or at least questioned, but if I told him, he might not want to go and we needed him to go. Against my better judgment, I decided not to tell him, as my family in Ukraine was very desperate.

I took a big breath of relief when the transaction was completed and no one suffered any untoward consequences. Of course, these days you go to your friendly Western Union or financial place and can transfer money internationally in a matter of a few minutes. That detailed description is just a glimpse into what my life would be for the next two years. All night long, I would write letters to everybody (congressmen, senators, and presidents in Russia and here), and during the day I would work at my OHSU residency and raise my two kids! Thank God again for my parents!

As I said previously, I made numerous appeals to government officials, and they responded with understanding and honest responses of sympathy for my situation. But one congressman, Les AuCoin, stood out among others. He took his job of serving his constituents much further. He took on my cause as a personal issue, and as he says in his book *Catch and Release*, he agreed to help even though he did not know how, but one thing he knew for sure was that if he didn't succeed, it wouldn't be for the lack of trying.

You see, at that time Congressman Les AuCoin was a chairman of the Defense Appropriations Subcommittee, and he rubbed shoulders with very important people in the Soviet government on a high level. A lot of information at that time was classified (including the name of his counterparts), but there was no way I would've known that at the time. Then one week I heard that a very important person from the Soviet government by the name of Georgi Arbatov would be speaking at Lewis & Clark College about a sister-cities exchange, economic benefits, etc. I had no way of knowing that Les AuCoin was establishing connection via Arbatov for my brother's benefit. Arbatov was the closest person to Gorbachev and was planning to meet with Les AuCoin that afternoon. I did not know any of that!

I went to Lewis & Clark College, and in the middle of the Q&A session, I asked Arbatov the most embarrassing question about human rights and the rights of my brother in particular. His face became burgundy angry, and after the lecture, he told me (in Russian) that I should've asked him my question in Russian and after the meeting. I also did not know that Les AuCoin's aide was in the audience, and after the session with Arbatov, the aide went straight to the airport to meet Congressman AuCoin and bring him to the Hilton for a private meeting with Arbatov. When the aide picked up AuCoin at the airport, he delivered some unwelcome news: "Raisa almost started World War III during the meeting." To make matters worse, when Arbatov was doing an interview on TV with one of the local stations, my brother's name came up again!

Les AuCoin not only put his heart toward my plight, but his family became involved as well. His daughter, Stacy AuCoin, carried a letter in her purse intended for a very high Soviet official and one day was able to meet him and pass on the letter. That might've played a crucial role, but I didn't know until later. When I heard what she did, I exclaimed, "You did what?!" This was behind the Iron Curtain time!!! The AuCoin family became a big part of our family. Anyway, for years, day and night we fought together, and then we heard the sweet sound of success! Naum was released from prison, and shortly after, he and his family were permitted to leave Ukraine and come to the USA.

In October 1988 Congressman Les AuCoin, his daughter, Stacy (or, as my brother affectionately called her, Anastasia, like in Russian), and I flew to New York to bring Chernobelsky's family to their new home in Portland, Oregon. When we were approaching the Portland airport, we heard the captain announce over the loudspeaker: "Ladies and gentleman, we have on this plane Naum Chernobelsky and family who are arriving to their new home in Portland with the distinguished, honorable Congressman Les AuCoin. Let's welcome them to their new home!" The plane erupted in applause, and I cried endless tears of release, happiness, joy, and victory! An emotional rapture! They were free and here!!! The airport was full of relatives with flowers as well as every TV station and newspaper reporters looking for an interview... It was glistening with joy and happiness and love!

At last, home, sweet home!

14

THE UNFORGETTABLE FIRST VISIT TO THE HOLY LAND IN 1988

IN 1988 ISAAK AND I HAD BEEN IN THE COUNTRY ALMOST EIGHT YEARS IN our beautiful Pacific Northwest, USA. Isaak's birthday was coming up in March. What a glorious birthday present it would be if we could travel. We both loved traveling, but we had not had the chance to do it! So in March of 1988, we decided that we wanted to go to Israel and the Holy Land. It had been a dream of mine and Isaak's for so many years. When we had been in Italy during emigration, we were so close to Israel, but we could not even dream about it for obvious financial and logistical reasons.

The decision was made, and I went to a small travel agency nearby that I had heard was very reasonable, I met a nice agent, Laura, and told her about our long-time fascination with Israel and also that we had a fascination with Europe, especially

France and England. We thought that if we were going to fly that long, maybe we could visit Europe as well. France especially was glorified in Russian literature, and French was a language of royalty for Pierre in *War and Peace*... Anyway, we dreamed of walking Champs-Élysées Avenue and seeing the Eiffel Tower and Montparnasse. The price of the trip was very important for us, trying to do it in the most economical way. I remember that we were still sleeping on the beds and mattresses that had been donated to us by another family. Other immigrants would buy expensive furniture at the first chance they had, but we decided that we could sleep on the ones we had and instead travel.

So, I was at the travel agency, and Laura loved me and I loved her style. She was going to get me on the most economical but inclusive trip. We were looking at two packages for Israel, and Paris and England. The brochure she showed me would spend fourteen days in the Holy Land. I read it, and it looked good. The description had everything—Jerusalem, Tel Aviv, Tiberias, Masada, the Yad Vashem Holocaust memorial and museum, the Dead Sea, and Eilat. It looked good, and we were super excited! Anticipation and joy were off the scale!

Sometime in the beginning of March 1988, we set off for our adventure. Everything from flying on the EL AL plane to landing in that mysterious, beloved land was an incredible experience of a lifetime! When we were on the plane, I observed Orthodox Jews putting on a tefillin (a prayer box placed on the forehead and leather straps on the forearm to signify closeness and connection to Hashem/God)! Watching that ritual and prayer took me back to my childhood when I watched my grandpa praying behind the closed door and curtain. (God forbid someone see him praying?) And here—high, very high in the sky on a plane that I am sure was carrying people of many different religions and faiths—a small group of Orthodox Jews was praying in open sight!!! Like I said, my absolute awe started on that plane. And the feeling of stepping off that plane into that Holy Land was also beyond description. Even though I am not a Bible scholar, I knew some verses and some stories, and a lot of them happened there and I was standing there!!! Deep emotions enveloped me, like a kaleidoscope of happiness and sorrow, laughter and tears, sadness and joy, excitement and anticipation, deep yearning for the beautiful and sometimes unreachable—all the colors of the rainbow of the world, history, and Adonai! Even with all adjectives in the world, I won't be able to do justice to the incredible feeling that consumed my mind and body. *Unforgettable* does not explain the depth of what I felt!

We joined a group of people on a large bus where the majority of people were from England and Germany. Our tour guide gave all her commentary in English and German. The American representation on the bus was a single guy from Nebraska (his wife refused to go); a nice black couple from Kansas City, Kansas; and me and Isaak. Even later, when our guide gave us a puzzling look and asked us if we were Jewish and we said yes, she asked why we were on this tour. Almost halfway through, we realized that we are on a very Christian tour to Israel. It did not matter. We were still walking through history!

On Isaak's birthday, March 10, we were sitting in a small white-linen table café and having some coffee and sweets to celebrate. All of a sudden, a bomb squad car pulled in, and the soldiers cleared us in one minute. We did not understand what they were saying, and the owner told us to get away at least twenty meters. We watched them remove a brown bag from the table next to where we had been sitting. They suspected it was a bomb—unfortunately, that was at the beginning of an uprising with suicide bombers. A few minutes later, the café was full of laughter and life and joy again. Like I said nothing could spoil our awe of the country!

Climbing Masada, taking a boat ride in the Tiberian Sea (the place of the loaves and fish miracle), enjoying Tel Aviv's big cosmopolitan city with beautiful museums, and taking in Yad Vashem were all incredibly moving experiences. At the memorial monument, when you first enter, you walk through the Avenue of the Righteous, with trees planted labeled with names of people and countries that helped and hid Jews during the war. Then the most sad experience for me (and of course all of it is sad just thinking what one human being did to others), with lots of tears and heartache, was the visit to the Children in the Holocaust exhibit in the museum! You walk in a completely dark room in the shape of a globe, and in the middle and on the walls are numerous candles (electric, of course). And all the time that you walk in that darkness, a very solemn, deep voice is reading names and ages and countries where children were taken from and later perished in the Holocaust. Shivers and tears I felt just thinking that such atrocities happened to all those innocent children, and the WORLD WAS SILENT!!! Innocent souls lost forever. Crying did not bring me any relief, just the deepest sadness and sorrow. Grief brings a new meaning to the phrase "Never again"! It goes to that deep emotional center in your heart!

Then we went to Jerusalem, which is definitely a one-of-a-kind city, not only because the whole city was built from white stone. *Biblical* and *deeply spiritual* are how I would describe it. When you get to the Western Wall, the emotion—the connection—you experience is like nowhere in the world. When I first stopped and touched the wall, it was like an out-of-body experience. An electrical current passed through me (not literally)—the emotions, everything, penetrates your whole being, and it's just beyond words to describe it.

Just slightly jumping ahead—since that time, I have been to Israel five times now and know most of the sites, but that feeling that I had at the Western Wall returns to me every time I touch this sacred place! I also put a small piece of paper in the wall asking GOD for something that was desperately needed. Something really significant. It is a very common ritual, and lots of people do it. There are millions of papers in the wall. I asked for two very important things, and they both came true. Sounds childish or naïve, but it works and only there. Miracle from God? It is.

So once again the tour was Christian, and we walked in the steps of Jesus, but I found it interesting and an unforgettable experience. I felt pure amazement for the country that was so young, barely forty years old and managed to achieve so much.

Truly the country that was built on thousands and thousands of years of history! God's given land!

One person from England in my group was a retired tailor, and it just so happened that he had been born and lived in the same area of Ukraine as I did (it was Poland then). He had been drafted to the army, and just before the war he escaped from the army via China and other countries and British-mandated land of future Israel and then to London. Fifty years later, he was celebrating what he called his "great escape" and tracing down all the steps of his escape! We were standing at the highest point in Jerusalem, and he said: "I was standing in this very spot fifty years ago, and all you could see then were swamps! Of course now that it has been turned into a beautiful, blooming garden, everybody wants it!"

And of course, I need to end this chapter with another funny story. In the hotels where we were housed, there was always a beautiful (to me, anyway—as the saying goes, all in the eye of the beholder), lavish buffet. The Israeli breakfast is very bountiful and very big. It's a standard, not just for tourists. That is how I grew up in Ukraine. For breakfast we would have food that is not considered very breakfast-like here or in other countries. Not your average American or continental breakfast! There was a gentleman in our group who was traveling solo, so he frequently dined with us at the same table. He was from Nebraska and did not know or had never seen some of the stuff on that buffet. He would go through the line between me and Isaak and usually would take what we took, especially on the food that he did not know. You see, I grew up eating herring (pickled fish), often for breakfast with a salad of tomato, cucumber, and onion. Israelis do that too. Also very tasty olives, feta cheese, other cheeses, and yogurt. The pastries and bread were so very good. And there were of course boring cereals and granola bars. Sorry, never learned to like those for breakfast?

So one day I went through the buffet excited about the food, and Rick was behind me. He saw me take a spoonful of herring from the big bowl, and he asked, "What is this?" and I replied, "Pickled fish." He obviously had never seen it and, seeing me take a spoonful, he did the same. Then potatoes and then crunchy cucumber. We got to our table and started eating. Rick took a first bite of the herring, and I saw him turning purple. No, he was not choking, but he just could not swallow it. He turned away and spit it out in a napkin, and just softly said, "If my wife only knew what I eat here!" Yes, herring—especially in the morning—is definitely an acquired taste. You either like it or you don't, and there is no middle ground. You really have to grow up with it. That nice man from Nebraska will remember that breakfast for a long time!

I've already expressed in many different ways how much I enjoyed the trip and everything about it. I loved Israel so much that I was determined to send my parents—who did not travel at all—to Israel! In May of 1992, I found a Russian-speaking tour in Israel and sent them there! My father was nicknamed Gorbachev, as his first name was the same, Mikhail. They had the time of their lives! An unforgettable experience! On their return, they talked about Israel all the time. Unfortunately, my father passed away in August of 1992, but I am so happy that he got to see it! What an incredible land—you literally walk on history!

15

MY FATHER'S STORY!

My dear father, Mikhail Chernobelsky, was the youngest of six children (three brothers and three sisters), born on May 20, 1916, in a small shtetl (village) of Lozovatoye, Vinnytsia Oblast, Ukraine. The family was very poor, and with six kids, they barely made ends meet. His father was a small mill operator. My father's documents showed him as five years older so he could help his father in the mill. So essentially he started working at eleven or twelve years of age. I am sure that he was also doing other jobs. He probably was a shoe-repair apprentice because later in life, he always repaired our shoes and did a great job of it. So, life was difficult. His mother died when he was sixteen, so the older sisters kind of assumed motherly roles for him.

When the war started, all three brothers became soldiers and fought for the USSR starting in 1941. My father was twenty-five. He fought in the war from 1941 to 1945. He saw a lot of death, injuries, heartbreak, tears, and loss of love and loved ones. As he was fighting all those years, he was in some serious battles and caught a few bullets in his left shoulder and his leg. His two older brothers were killed in action during the war!

And then in 1944 when the war was taking a turn toward the Soviet Union's victory, my father was in Czechoslovakia marching to Berlin, but he got separated from his battalion and was taken by Germans as a prisoner. I'm not sure about the details of his captivity, but he repeated this one episode many times for all of us. And that story was about a large group of Armenians who essentially saved my father's life. He felt incredibly grateful for that! So, when he was captured, the Germans ordered all the prisoners to strip their clothes. He just by chance happened to be next to the Armenian soldiers. My father was dark-skinned and looked like them. When he stripped, the German soldier pointed a gun at his privates saying: "*Jude*" (sounds like "yuda," meaning "Jew") because my father was circumcised. All the Armenian soldiers surrounded him and said: "No, he is Armenian." The German soldier was not satisfied and asked him to speak to the Armenian in their dialect, which my dad did not know. So, once again shielding him, they all said in one voice that he was taken away when he was very small and never learned how to speak. That saved him! Also luckily, right before capture, he'd buried his documents, including his Soviet Army ID, which would've said *Jewish* as a nationality?!!!

A few days later, he managed to escape from that prison, and then after running for a while, he was extremely exhausted and hungry, so he took a chance and knocked at the first door he came to in a little village, asking for shelter and food, and the family took him in. Unfortunately, I never learned the name of the family or the name of the village. I just remember that whenever my father talked about them, it was with great warmth and care. He always told us how nicely they treated him. "They treated me as if I was their own son." At the time I heard it, that was just a nice story of capture, survival, escape, finding a nice home and being treated very nicely, and then finally rejoining the army and returning home! As they say, a nice fairy tale, but that part of my father's life would enter mine much later... Coincidence? I don't believe in coincidences. We are all connected—if not by blood, often by circumstances!

I reviewed my father's records from the Memory of the People website. It's like Ancestry.com only for Russian military personnel. My father enlisted on July 16, 1941, in the city of Odessa, Ukraine. The next notification says that he was killed on March 8, 1942, and buried in a mass grave in the village of Borisovka, Rostovskaya Oblast. Then an October 13, 1944, says he was missing in action. That was probably when he was captured and imprisoned. The place of MIA was listed as Poland. Then yet another document stated that a correction was made to the previous MIA document and that he was imprisoned and released. The date of separation listed is October 11, 1944. He returned and reenlisted in 1945 and was released from duties from Battalion 610 on July 5, 1945.

I was born after the war, but the war was under my father's skin. We grew up listening to the heartbreaking stories of love lost, life lost or changed forever, and wounds (both physical and emotional). A lot of those were set to songs. Our whole family loved singing, and my mother and my brother had beautiful voices. So our favorite pastime was listening to them singing those songs after dinner.

My father taught my daughter (who was four or five then) one of those songs. Sometimes as she grew up I would ask her if she remembered, and she did. Then her daughter got interested when the meaning of the song was translated to her, and she wanted to learn it too. So my father's story lives through generation in his songs. That was a very beautiful, nostalgic story! Just recently I was driving and started to sing that song to myself, but I could not remember all the words. I stopped and called my daughter, and after forty years she reminded me of the words! I believe that it was my dad reaching out from heaven to us! My father was a very gentle, loving person. I learned my hugs and kisses from him. It did not have to be a special occasion—he always had hugs and kisses for us kids and for other relatives and friends!

He passed away from a brief illness and complications of a stroke on August 22, 1992. He was very ill on my birthday on August 19, but my mom wrote a birthday card and put it in his hand to give it to me. He handed the card to me, not able to talk. I still have that card twenty-eight years later! He was seventy-six years old when he died. I do not like to celebrate my birthday anymore since it always reminds me of that bitter time of loss.

I keep his gentle loving soul in my heart forever, and I believe he is still watching over us and we occasionally connect through songs and memories. And I have a grandson who is named for him, my sweet Michael! What a beautiful loving soul he is. Just like his great-grandfather that he is named after!

16

MY MOTHER'S STORY

MY DEAR MOTHER, ANNA (ANYA) GENDLER, WAS BORN ON JANUARY 21, 1924, in the small village of Bershad, Ukraine. She was the second daughter in the family. Her sister, Manya, was three years old at that time. My grandpa Itzhak Gendler was not very happy, as he'd always wanted a son.

My mom was born in poverty, and that is how her young years were remembered. From a very young age she helped at home with different chores (cooking, cleaning, sewing…). She had two younger brothers, Josef who was born in 1926 and Lazar who was born in 1929. Life made another unfortunate turn, and at the age of fifteen my mother was forced to assume the mother role for her younger siblings.

Her teen years started with the devastation of the war, hunger worse than ever, and living under German occupation in a ghetto. She started working for the city in the vital statistics department at age eighteen. All documents at that time were handwritten, and she had beautiful handwriting. Her older sister went to a larger city, lived with relatives, and studied to become a teacher. So, as I said, my mom became a mother to her two younger brothers. She also had a rather mean-spirited stepmother who had two more kids with my grandpa (a son in 1936 and a daughter in 1938; the son died in infancy). My mother's memories of her stepmother were rather bitter. That woman would frequently lock the three stepkids outside the house in the bitter cold, and they had to sit together and warm each other until my grandpa showed up from work, usually late at night. Sometimes neighbors would take them in, feeling sorry for the kids, and when my grandpa returned from work they would say to him, "What kind of woman treats children that way?" So it was very obvious that my mom never got the love and warmth that every child deserves! Maybe that was why she was never a hugger, as she did not get any hugs herself? In 1941 my mom truly became a mother to her two brothers, as the stepmother evacuated with her daughter, Dina, after her son, Volodya, passed away from some childhood disease. Before that my mom had endured six years of that mean-spirited stepmother!

She was a great daughter and loving sister to her younger brothers. Unfortunately, the youngest one Lazar (Lenya) passed away in my mother's arms in 1943. He had meningitis, and no treatment was available. He was thirteen at the time. She was still holding him in her embrace when her father got home. My grandpa—in a rash of grief—beat my mom like it was her fault that this horrible thing happened! She talked about her brother in the most loving, endearing terms. She told us that even at a young age, he was such a dreamer. She said that he was very interested in astrology just by looking at the sky. He would wonder and say that the stars are so beautiful and it would be interesting to see when in the future people would reach those stars and planets, moon, Mars, Venus, and make some wonderful discoveries! He was fascinated with our cosmos and probably would've became a scientist or an astronaut. He was a dreamer!

The other brother, Josef, joined the Soviet Army immediately after turning eighteen in 1944. My mom begged him not to go and even told him that she could make his records show him a year younger to avoid it (as she worked in vital statistics). But he was a big patriot and had to go to defend his country. He told my mom that if she even attempted to do it, he would report her to the authorities. He enlisted in 1944, and just few short months later, in East Prussia, the tank that he was in hit a minefield and exploded at the end of 1944. He was buried in a mass grave in that area.

That my mother survived the German occupation was a miracle by itself. Mom described how many times she was chased and beaten by Romanian police/collaborators. The houses were randomly raided, and people would try to hide in underground storage areas. My mom would sit in a chair on the carpet covering the trap door and wonder if she would be the next casualty. You see, she would get nervous attacks of hiccups when she went underground and worried that she would endanger other people there. So she never hid. The Germans were leaving rather in a hurry, but being defeated and angry, they had to do their last "deeds" of taking people out randomly from their homes and killing them.

Before we left the Soviet Union in 1979, we traveled with my mom to the small city of Bershad in Ukraine and visited the cemetery. Mom pointed to the different graves and said, "Those were our neighbors on the right and those on the left..."

After the war, both my mom and dad were married briefly to other spouses and divorced shortly after. (I did not know that until I got married!) How my mom and dad met, I don't know. I never asked? I am sure that they found common ground in having survived the horrors of the war, then brief and failed marriages... They got married in 1947, and in 1948 my brother, Naum, was born.

My mom was the best mom in the world. Her main priority in life was to provide for her children. She wanted us to have everything that she had not been able to have. My mom worked a full-time job, but on her days off, it was cooking and cooking and baking! Boy, was Mom a great cook. We all took it for granted, as she always cooked with great love and in abundance for us kids and later grandkids. There was no better job for her than to cook dinner for all of us. I used to give her long lectures about obesity, hypertension, diabetes, cholesterol...but how do I miss her cooking now!!! That was her true expression of love. Even though she was not big on hugging and kissing, she put all her love and efforts into preparing great food for us and buying nice clothes. The day that Mom stopped cooking was the day I knew that she was very ill! She baked such incredibly good stuff as Napoleons, strudels, the best apple cake, walnut and honey cake, Prague chocolate cake, cookies, and freshly baked bread! Everything from scratch! And cooking! I do not know where to start! It was all so tasty.

There was a lady in town that my mom baked for on occasion. She really loved her Napoleons and strudels and so encouraged me to get recipes (which my mom never had—a pinch of that and a pinch of this). After my mom passed away, the lady searched different Russian and Jewish delis to find something similar, but she never did! I also learned after Mom passed away that she had cooked and baked for the neighbors next door (when grandkids had turned to pizza and hot dogs and did not want Grandma's cooking to smell up their T-shirts). The neighbors, who owned and operated a deli in downtown Portland, said that they had never had such tasty food. They brought me some pots and pans and baking forms, and I asked them to keep them. Cooking was her main purpose. She finally was not hungry anymore and wanted to make sure that everybody was taken care of!

My mom had been ill from a very young age. At thirty-five she became blind in one eye as a complication of very severe hypertension. As a child of five or six, I would walk with my mom to the market, and all of a sudden she would collapse, and I would run to a policeman and cry that my mom was down, and they would call an ambulance. Maybe that was why I wanted to be a doctor from a very early age?! The last year, she was really ill, but with help we were able to keep her at home, and she passed away in her own bed in her apartment. At the end, she hallucinated and saw her youngest brother, and she would ask me to go to the kitchen and give him a bun. She said: "He is very hungry." Once you live through hunger, you never forget! When she shopped, she always wanted to buy in large quantities so she would not run out!

She passed away on April 18, 2002. She was not able to talk as a result of her strokes, and we were all there surrounding her. She looked at all of us. I was holding her hand, and all of a sudden her eyes were going from side to side, like she was reading a most fascinating book. She was reading a book of her LIFE! I just said, "It's okay, Mom," and she took her last breath! She was seventy-eight.

A few years before Mom died, she was determined to become a citizen of the USA. She studied with tutors and seriously prepared for the test. She was completely blind in one eye and walked with a cane. She was ill, and I am sure that her doctor would've given her a letter of excuse because of her state of health! She did not want to hear about it. My son, who was a sophomore in high school and loved studying history, told me that Grandma was better prepared than he was! She knew all one hundred questions and passed! It was a day of celebration!

And that brings me to the story of the hummingbird (and the name of my book), which is again a little jump ahead in time for a moment. My views on science and what happens in the afterlife have changed considerably. I am a strong believer that when the PHYSICAL BODY DIES, THE SOUL goes on in some shape or form, and if the time is right, it comes back to us loved ones. We just need to be willing to see it!

So, when my sweet Isaak passed away rather unexpectedly on November 28, 2012, needless to say, I was alone, devastated, and heartbroken! The depression was very deep. My days consisted of crying most of the time, but I forced myself to get out of my big home and walk around no matter what the weather was. I did that on a cold day in February of 2013. It was very cold! I just got out of the house, and right across the street on a tree, I saw this incredible little bird sparkling with bright red and green. I am not a birder, and at the time I did not know much about hummingbirds, but I knew that they are very fast and usually don't stay in one spot for a long time.

That little bird was sitting there and looking at me. I stopped, tears rolling down my cheeks, and I began talking to this little bird and sobbing. I said, "Mom, is it you? I know that you've seen my sweet Isaak, and I am sure you prepared a table for him there just like you did in life. He always liked your cooking and baking. Please, take care of him." That went on for probably ten or fifteen minutes. I was sobbing, and a man with a dog came by and saw me talking to a tree and asked if I was okay. I said yes, and he left, and the little bird was still there. Since then, whenever I walk, a hummingbird hovers over me. Even when I do not see it, I hear the call.

I also learned that in Oregon there are two types of hummingbirds, rufous and Anna's. The rufous migrates for winter, but the Anna's stays here. Anna is my mom's name! She is still hovering over me forever!

17

9/11/2001

Life is good! Portland is clean and beautiful and green (just like my grandma described). Our daughter, Lilya, received her master of business degree (MBA) from DePaul University and married a wonderful young man, Chad, who we love very much. They married in a beautiful ceremony at the Oregon Golf Club in April 2000. My mom, though she was very ill at the time, lived to see and participate in the wedding. David, our son, graduated from Wilson High School and was now in his second year at Portland State University.

Isaak and I were both professionals working good jobs and traveling a lot. Life was really good, and suddenly...

I remember the moment I saw the tragedy on TV and felt complete disbelief. Did I mix up the channels? Is this an action movie? I remember that I was getting ready to go to work, and the TV was on, and while I was getting ready I was listening to the news in the background. It caught my full attention, and without realizing what was happening, I just froze and watched two planes—one after the other—fly into one building and the next building, and both towers began to collapse like they were made of sand! Complete and total disbelief! The Twin Towers collapsed and reduced to a mountain of ash? What did I just see? I had that gut feeling that it was something horrible, but I still did not know what! My mom was watching too and attempted to talk to me and ask some questions, but I snapped at her...I was not sure what to say.

I left for work, and only marginally understanding the tragedy, I cried bitterly all the way to work. I barely completed my day at work and then came back home and immediately glued my eyes to a TV set. When I heard an explanation of what had happened, I still could barely comprehend the hatred and loss of life, the unbelievable size and effect of this tragedy, and all I was able to feel for the next month or so was despair, emptiness, anger, and grief for this beautiful new home of mine, the USA. My home was tragically violated. People who senselessly died entered deep into my soul. I grieved deeply for the country for lost lives.

I was overcome by this overwhelmingly sad feeling that it would never be the same again! Innocence lost! Travel certainly changed a great deal and probably forever.

Then the war in Iraq began, and my son-in-law, Chad, was called to duty by the army to go to Iraq on a mission to capture Saddam Hussein. He was a third-year emergency room resident stationed at Fort Hood in Killeen, Texas, close to Austin.

He left for Iraq in 2003 when their son, Michael, was just three months old!!!!

It was an extremely difficult time of waiting and praying for his safe return every day!

When he came back, he never talked about his experiences, but from a few very subtle comments, I understood that he lived through some horrific experiences. Some might've been incredible for an ER doctor to see and do, but undoubtedly some were so heartbreaking and traumatizing to see—twentysomethings losing both legs while sitting on a toilet as the grenade just exploded under them or doing an open heart massage on a critically wounded soldier.

Chad injured his own back when he needed to jump off the cote he was on as an RPG was flying toward their tent. One picture of a thermometer on the tent said 138 degrees Fahrenheit. One time he was in the back of the van in full gear on a Saddam Hussein–capturing mission, and he wrote, "I sweated in places I did not know that I had."

Then, thank God, he returned home, and it was shortly after a Fourth of July celebration, end of summer. His mom was there when he returned. The neighboring kids were playing with leftover firecrackers, and when he heard the sound, he immediately ordered his wife and his mother to take cover under the bed, as I am sure he had to do many times from threats of RPGs and other ammunition! I am sure that those sounds stayed with him for a while. I hope and pray that he is clear of them now!

What extreme hate can do. Change the country, change the world, change the way we travel, and give birth to more hate?!

When I write this, I cannot help but think of John Lennon's so very popular song "Imagine" and wish for world peace.

Hate is so powerful, but so is love! I choose to believe that life and love and peace will prevail!!!!

18

THE STORY OF ISAAK—2004

IN A PREVIOUS CHAPTER I TOLD YOU THAT AFTER ISAAK AND I FINALLY MET IN 1971 or 1972 and kissed under those magical grapes on the Black Sea, we both returned to our respective places of work and school but felt that we wanted to be in touch. That is how our postal romance started.

I left for Chelyabinsk, Ural Mountains in Russia to go to my medical school, and Isaak went back to the city of Vinnytsia in Ukraine to get back to his work.

One month later we both ended up in the hospital at the same time—me in Chelyabinsk with a classic full-blown case of rheumatic fever and Isaak Vinnytsia with the autoimmune disease of arthritis. We were both rather ill and did not have much to do, and the only way to keep communication going was via letters.

When my grandkids will read that, I am not sure that they will understand. Letters? No cell phone? No FaceTime? Impossible, but true.

Very warm, romantic letters and just talking through them. We were slowly but definitely falling in love. I was nineteen, and Isaak was twenty-one.

My grandma Khasya at age seventy left her very comfortable home in a mild and warm-temperature climate in Odessa at the Black Sea, where people were still sunbathing and swimming in September. She came to Chelyabinsk where the temperature began to dip into minus digits. As a matter of fact, the very first thing I had to learn in Chelyabinsk was to put goose fat on my cheeks so I wouldn't get frostbite while walking a short distance from home to catch a bus to school. I also needed to learn how to walk in those special wool boots (*Valenki*), which were very warm but were rounded on the bottom and unsteady, and it took me time to adjust and learn.

My parents were working and were not able to come when I was ill, and everybody I knew—including the owners of the house where I was renting a room and where my grandma stayed—was amazed that my grandma left her home and came to be with me. When I told that to my mom, she just responded, "She owes me that!" The air was smelling with secrets, but I was too young and too careless to know or to care. And then I had twenty-six more years to ask about it, and I did not! I so wish that I would have!

So Grandma cooked for me. Also, on the way to Chelyabinsk, she'd stopped in Moscow and brought me a pineapple and a few bananas from there. That was the first time that I ate those, I think. After one month in the hospital and being rather ill, I returned home and started my recovery. The letters were flowing between Isaak and me almost every day. One day Grandma and I went to the post office together, and when I picked up my few letters—"love letters"—the anticipation and romance caused me to be very excited and somewhat shaky. Grandma took one look at me and matter-of-factly said, "You love him. Yes, you two will get married!" The seed was planted.

I was finishing up my first year and taking an academic year off after that. Isaak and I had plans to meet while I would be on academic leave. And we did, and the rest is history. He came to my town to see my parents and ask for my hand, and he took me to a carnival in town. He said, "If I win at the target shooting, will marry me?" That is how Isaak proposed! I was a good target shooter, but I lost. Did I intentionally lose, or was he a better shot?? He probably was a better shot, but I would have married him anyway. Beautiful, big wedding courtesy of my parents. Incredibly good time with so many people being a part of our union! Great ceremony. We looked so young and handsome and beautiful! We were young! I was twenty-one, and Isaak was twenty-three.

Because of circumstances, we never had a honeymoon, but we were so much in love—more every day! Our whole life was a honeymoon! No, of course it was not, and we had missteps and glitches, which we were able to resolve in a loving, civil manner. Isaak, with his quiet voice and unassuming presentation, was a voice of reason and such an ultimate peacemaker! He always had a nice, quiet explanation and amazingly was able to cool down my hot head. He had the ultimate goodness of Pisces, and that was his horoscope sign.

So when our twenty-fifth anniversary was approaching in 1998, we decided to finally have a honeymoon and splurge on a good one. We ended up going to Australia, New Zealand, and Fiji! What an amazing trip it was! The trip included three days in Fiji—what a beautiful piece of paradise! Then two weeks in Australia snorkeling the Great Barrier Reef, flying in a helicopter around Ayers Rock, taking the legendary *Ghan* train ride to Alice Springs, and visiting the incredible cities of Sydney and Melbourne. Then two weeks in New Zealand at the unforgettable and very scenic Milford Sound, with visits to both North and South Islands. Being a part of the regatta in Auckland and sheering sheep. Like I said before, the trip was a dream, and it more than made up for not having an original honeymoon.

Just to look back for a minute. In 1998 when we started thinking about the trip, we were both very busy professionals. Traditionally, I would be in charge of organizing all trips, but this one was longer and a bit more complicated and involved communicating with a travel agency in Canada, all of which required more time and effort. Then one day I angrily said to Isaak that it was his anniversary too and he could help me! I was my "bubbly" loud self. This quiet, even-hearted man replied: "Why? I would only be in the way and you would redo it your way anyway." That beautiful soul of Isaak, who never yelled or even used a loud voice, but he was right again! Isaak was very wise, good at judging character, and big-hearted. That heart carried a great love for me, our children, family, and friends. He always strove for peace with everyone and everywhere!

So back to that unforgettable trip. We were in Australia and on a bus to go see the main attraction, Ayers Rock. Our tour guide asked about how many people wanted to climb the rock, and twenty-five signed up (including me), but then after she described how difficult that hike was, how many people fell and were injured or died, only one guy remained on the list. The rest of us did what they call Chicken Rock and got our certificates for climbing. We also took a helicopter that we thought would take us over Ayers Rock, but it was *around* the rock, as it's a sacred Aboriginal site and flying over the rock was forbidden. That was the first time we flew in a helicopter! The day was very hot, and the rock was in the middle of the desert, and when we boarded the bus tired and thirsty, we were soon in for a very nice surprise.

Our bus had been driving for a very short distance when it stopped. We stepped out, still in the desert in the view of the rock, and were greeted with champagne and mimosas and orange juice! The cold drinks were very welcoming. Then we saw ten beautiful tables with white tablecloths and a lavish buffet right there in the middle of the desert. A musician was playing a didgeridoo (a national musical instrument, which looks like a long bassoon). Magical, beautiful view of Ayers Rock, soft music, and delicious food, and then at dusk an astronomer with a telescope explained all the stars and constellations! So, once again, the trip was amazing, and I am so glad that we did not wait for our retirement before I could travel together with Isaak to four continents!

Returning to Isaak's state of health. Just a quick travel back to 1995. Isaak was working as a computer programmer for this private company, and he was forty-five and very active in playing and loving many sports. During lunchtime at work one day, he called some of his coworkers (ages ranging from twenty to twenty-five) for a competition in push-ups. He did fifty of those nonstop and won the contest, beating all those kids and even getting a certificate. I still have it twenty-five years later.

About a week later, Isaak began to cough and feel shortness of breath. I thought that he had pneumonia, but when—for the first time in my life—I listened to his lungs and heart, I heard a very loud heart murmur that I never knew he had?! That very day, he was going to see his doctor, and the same day he was admitted to the hospital and diagnosed with IHSS (idiopathic hypertrophic subaortic stenosis). It's a congenital heart disease, but it had not been diagnosed at birth, only after exertion forty-five years later. Now he had to limit most of his sport activities such as soccer, volleyball, floor hockey, basketball, and weight lifting, definitely push-ups. We still walked a lot and he was managing okay. He swam occasionally. But then in 2003 and the beginning of 2004, he began to experience what seemed to be an exacerbation of arthritis. He would get swollen-ankle pain but later cough and sob, and his doctor, knowing of his heart defect, unfortunately misdiagnosed him with a heart disease called diastolic dysfunction.

Isaak began treatment with diuretics, but unfortunately he was not getting better. Because even though he did have a congenital heart defect, it was not his heart this time. Unfortunately, his autoimmune lung disease would not be diagnosed until 2007...

19

THANKSGIVING WILL NEVER BE THE SAME

IN AUGUST 2007, RIGHT AROUND THE TIME OF MY AND MY DAUGHTER'S birthdays, and as my daughter and her family were moving to Portland from Texas, Isaak was feeling progressively worse in spite of the treatment for his "heart condition," which was obviously not helping. We'd already purchased a pulse oximeter (the little instrument that measures the oxygen level in blood). He was noted to have low readings like in the upper eighties (88 or 89 percent) in the office but was still being treated for a heart condition??? Treated for that since 2004?

At that time Isaak was working as a computer manager for the business center of Willamette Dental Group in Hillsboro, Oregon. I worked in a primary care clinic on another side of town in Southeast Portland. Right in the middle of the day, I got a call from Isaak, and he told me that he was feeling awful and his oxygen level was 84 percent, and it was hard to breathe so he was going to St. Vincent's hospital. It was my lunchtime, and I talked to the clinic manager to cancel all my afternoon appointments and met Isaak at the hospital ER.

He was having difficulty breathing, but when admitted to the hospital for a workup, he was still given Lasix (the diuretic that he had been on for three years by that point). We were also told that we were to wait for his primary care doctor to arrive to see him. For the first time in my life, I became confrontational and said that we were not waiting for anyone except a specialist to determine what was wrong with Isaak. I had to jump through some bureaucratic hoops and sign a number of papers. The bottom line was that the pulmonologist came in and scheduled Isaak for a bronchoscopy the next morning. He had the bronchoscopy done and was diagnosed with a rather rare autoimmune condition of idiopathic pulmonary fibrosis (IPF, usually a diagnosis of exclusion). Even as a practicing medical doctor, I did not know about it? Not much was available for treatment, and the prognosis was up to five years survival. Occasionally people might need a transplant. Isaak was just fifty-seven years old. Our daughter had just moved to town with two of our grandkids, who were two and four. Isaak was absolutely crazy in love with them.

That is when the race against the clock started, and we both were determined to beat that horrible disease! We were referred to the University of Washington Medical Center in Seattle, Washington, and were being seen there by a specialist in IPF. After multiple monthly trips to Seattle, a consult at the Mayo Clinic affiliate in Denver, Colorado, and multiple other attempts to help Isaak (too many to describe in three and a half years), he was getting progressively worse. Losing fifty-five pounds of weight and now being dependent on oxygen, he finally was put on a transplant list. That was now our only hope, and we were waiting for it as a panacea! Being on a transplant list meant that at any given day or night, we had to be within three hours from Seattle. So, for the next year and a half, we could no longer go to the beach, mountain, or any other places.

It was just lucky that maybe just two to three years before Isaak was placed on the transplant list, we had been able to travel. At that time Isaak had become dependent on oxygen at night and occasionally during the day. I came to his doctor and asked him if there was a way that Isaak would be able to travel (as you can't go on a plane with an oxygen tank). Initially the doctor told me that it was a crazy idea, but then he told me about an oxygen concentrator (a small machine in a leather case that looks like it is a video camera). That machine uses room air, enriches it, and turns it into 98 percent oxygen. It's completely compact and useful, can be recharged after six hours of continuous use, and with special arrangements with an airline can be allowed on the plane. I was happy to learn that because, as a primary care practitioner, I did not know about it? Believe it or not, we still traveled. Where did Isaak get the strength??? But we did, and he really wanted to see some national parks, and thanks to that source of oxygen, he was able to.

In 2008 we traveled with a group to the western national parks, Grand Canyon, Bryce Canyon, and Zion. This was a trip that we both had been looking forward to. Isaak was able to travel with the oxygen concentrator, and he was still very sensitive about people feeling sorry for him using oxygen, but at this point, he mainly used it at night. When we took it on a bus "just in case," the case looked like a camera case, and no one suspected anything. That was how he liked it.

So, there we were at Bryce Canyon, and it had a significant elevation (8,300 feet). High elevation and bad lungs do not agree. So, we arrived at the lodge and stopped there for lunch. As we were walking out of the bus and I was carrying the oxygen concentrator, Isaak said that I could leave it on the bus. I brought it anyway. Maybe after five minutes at the table just trying to decide what we would have for lunch, I noticed that Isaak's lips and fingernails had a blue tinge to them. Definite indication of lack of oxygen, I quickly turned on the oxygen concentrator and attached the tubing and nasal cannula, oxygen flowed, and the bluish tinge began to disappear! All attention was now on Isaak! I didn't care. Isaak tried to protest, but I told him it would be much more sad and embarrassing if he died.

For the rest of the trip, he was known as a man with oxygen. Then he stayed and breathed oxygen, and I ran quickly to the rim, took a few pictures, and came right back. By that time he'd recovered, oxygen in upper nineties, and now he was insisting that he wanted to walk to the rim too. I tried to tell him that he could just see the pictures, but in all honesty, pictures did not do it justice. So, he walked with me hand-in-hand, with the concentrator on my shoulder, to the canyon rim, and we got a picture by the sign saying, *Bryce Point, Elevation 8300!*

Then we were also scheduled to go to Peru, South America, the next year, but we changed it to the Amazon, as the disease had progressed and high elevation like in Peru would be deadly to his lungs. And the last trip we did together was to China in 2010. Honestly, I do not know how Isaak survived that one?! The flight was extremely difficult, and getting our "breathing machine" through all the security checks was an ordeal! Isaak, my architect at heart, really enjoyed seeing all the Olympics buildings in Beijing. Amazed by the Bird's Nest, one of the main buildings. At the Great Wall he climbed the first three steps then waited for me while I climbed the rest. Isaak truly enjoyed that trip!

When we got back, Isaak was becoming increasingly short of breath, and after many trips to Seattle, he ended up on a transplant list at the end of 2010 and beginning of 2011. We continued regular trips to Seattle to evaluate him for continuing eligibility for the transplant. He was briefly taken off the list because of his heart disease, and then after two cardio consults, he was put back on a list. Always be ready at a minute's notice! I got to work and carried my phone in my pocket. We had three "dry runs," which is when you are called to arrive and while you are driving like crazy, you are called again and told to turn back (usually because of a problem with the donor's lungs). One such call was when I was at work and had to leave my patient in the middle of a procedure, and my partner finished the visit for me. Then we were all the way to Olympia and we were told to turn around?! I've had some adrenalin rushes in my life. This one was absolutely exhausting. We came back and slept the rest of the day!

Finally, the day of surgery for a bilateral lung transplant arrived on October 15, 2012. Our family was all at the hospital. I flew in from Los Angeles, where I had been attending my cousin's funeral?!!! I made it in time to see Isaak before the surgery! After seven or eight hours of surgery (it was extremely complex, and of course I am not a surgeon, but even with the medical knowledge I had, it was still hard for me to understand all the intricacies of that complicated procedure).

Finally a doctor told us that there was an unforeseen complication with one of the donor's lungs, but the end result was good. The surgeon added that now it would be six weeks of ICU rehab and then six months living in Seattle for further rehabilitation. He also told us that Isaak's lungs were essentially gone, and he'd removed very scarred tissue that looked like two black rocks. Those lungs were not compatible with life!

We were all elated that Isaak got a new lease on life! We were elated! We all believed that he would be okay! We already knew of people who'd received the transplant and continued a rather normal life for ten to twenty-five years after.

Just a little step back. In my last job in the primary care clinic for twenty-six years, I never took sick time. So, when in the summer of 2012 Isaak mentioned that he'd had a few episodes of dizziness driving to his rehab twice a week at Meridian Hospital, I decided to take a month off in July for family sick leave to drive him to his rehabilitation appointments. He introduced me to the whole crew of volunteers that he socialized with, and they knew all about his grandkids that he was very proud off. We had lunches together in the cafeteria, and he told me about a kitchen worker who treated him very nice, etc. During that time we talked a lot about his illness, his transplant, and our future travel after recovering from the transplant. I was so very optimistically positive. Isaak was an ultimate optimist, but something that he said to me during that time showed that he was the only one who had some kind of premonition?? I told him not to be silly and that everything would be okay!!

So, Isaak's post-op course initially was great. He was recovering okay and was very eager to get better. His private nurse watched him have his first meal of grilled salmon, mashed potatoes, and asparagus, and she said that she had absolutely no doubt that Isaak would walk out of there in six weeks on his way to recovery!

I'd rented an apartment for us to stay in Seattle for his six months of rehabilitation. Isaak had the intubation removed and started speech therapy. (He even joked with the therapist, who wanted to encourage him to talk more as a practice. He said that he never talked much before so why start now?) And then he was feeling more tired and developed "dental" pain, but no problem was found. One day his physical therapist came at 10:00 a.m. and told him it was time to go for a hallway walk. Isaak tried to tell him that he was very tired, but everybody attributed that to deconditioning, and poor Isaak pushed himself from the strength reserves that he did not have anymore?! It was November 19, 2012. Not even halfway through the hallway walk, Isaak was turning blue and collapsed in a wheelchair that the PT guy was rolling behind him. He suffered a cardiac arrest! Watching his revival was surreal! When he got back, he looked at the clock, and it was 3:00 p.m. He somehow remembered that his PT was at 10:00. He looked at me and said, "Did I check out?" I smiled and said, "Big time."

Unfortunately, from that day on, his condition deteriorated rather fast. He was found to have a viremia (virus in the blood) with adenovirus. It's a simple cold virus that we all get with a winter cold, but it could be deadly to an immunocompromised individual. Isaak's medicines were adjusted, but the virus continued to multiply, oxygen fell, and he needed to be put in a medical coma.

We all said our goodbyes and asked him for his beautiful smile, and in spite being very ill, he left us all with that very friendly, handsome smile! He was placed in a rotational bed, and antiviral treatment started, but he only developed a side effect and his kidneys were shutting down. His new lungs were filling up with fluid every day, his oxygen was critically dropping, and he never came out of his coma.

On November 28, 2012, my angel joined other angels in heaven! We all saw orbs flying while we were sitting in the room. His nurse gave me a small bag with Isaak's beautiful hair, and in the future I deposited one small piece of it on each of my travels. So, my love, you did go with me to the remaining two continents! We all love you and miss you forever!

20

MY BUTTERFLY STORY!

IT WAS JANUARY OF 2013. EXTREMELY DARK TIME FOR ME. I DESCENDED into that black hole, the very sad time of grief and the place where I did not see a return from. The pain was so profound—excruciating, torturing—that it is impossible to describe with words. That heaviness and pain in my heart was wearing me down. Life absolutely had no meaning to me! I, normally a very social, outgoing person, was now very withdrawn, angry, and almost antisocial. I did not want to see anyone (even my own family, whom I love dearly). Even the emotions I experienced are hard to express by words! Everything was in black. My days were nights...I was lost and felt like I didn't want to live! For the first time in my life, I had suicidal thoughts, rather powerful ones. I stopped crossing bridges, as I frequently thought of jumping off one...

When I worked, I treated a lot of people for depression, but during that dark time, I realized that I had known very little about depression until it hit me.

Not only had I lost my best friend, the love of my life, my dear husband, Isaak, but I had also essentially lost half of me. I was "broken" and deeply depressed.

My daughter and her family—bless their hearts—came frequently from Seattle to try to cheer me up. She knew of my suicidal thoughts and was worried, but everything we did would bring tears and more sadness. She and her family surprised me once and came from Seattle with tickets to a Blazers game! I love the Blazers! But the whole game, I cried, as the only thing I remembered was how excited Isaak had been to take them all to a game when they first moved to town. The kids four and two. Michael at four became an instant fan!

The same thing happened when we all went to Mount Hood! It was beautiful, but all I remembered was when we had done that trip with Isaak. And I cried and cried! And my daughter might not have ever known this, but her last hard effort is what happened to save me. When she'd tried everything to cheer me up and it didn't work, she came to my room where I was crying and did not want to see anybody, and she bluntly told me that if I died by suicide, I would not be buried by Isaak! For the first time it "hit me." Yes, Lilucya, between that and my almost immediate travel after that, I was saved!

My daughter was my best psychologist. My friends and especially a couple that were in psychology and psychiatry insisted that I see a therapist, and I did, but that was a complete disaster. After crying my brain out in her office and telling her about my sweet love, Isaak, all she was able to do was give me two suggestions, and neither of them gave me hope! The first was that she could give me meditation and that I should do breathing exercises (which I couldn't do, as it only made me think more of how difficult it was for Isaak to breathe when his new lungs were filling up with the inflammatory fluid). The second was just a plain stupid statement: that in one hundred years, everyone I know and care about (including my grand-kids) will be dead. Even today, I struggle to understand how that was supposed to make me feel better. Needless to say, I never saw her or any other therapist again in my life. She came highly recommended from a good source, but her words definitely did not heal me. Words can heal, but they can harm as well.

The day was January 13, 2013. That was officially the first day of my retirement. It was an extremely cold winter day outside, and it was cold in my heart and soul. I thought that my son, David, would join me for a cup of tea. He had a last-minute invitation to a Blazers game and could not come.

So there I was by myself in that beautiful big home (designed by Isaak, as he had been an architect in Russia) that had been built just six years ago. Isaak's tender touch was in every door handle, counter, and drawer. But of course his biggest presence was still in my heart! I was sitting on a couch in a beautiful living room with twenty-foot ceilings and a gorgeous view of Mount Saint Helens but feeling that profound and painful sadness. All I could do was cry! Oceans of tears fell from my eyes...and suddenly, what was it? I saw some fluttering. In the right corner of the room, just above the TV, I saw some flickering. Was my vision going now? I wiped my tears. And I saw it! Very vividly.

The most beautiful—or I should say amazing—monarch (black and brown) butterfly! I knew that it was not a delusion. It was so real! I said: "Is that you, Isaak? I miss you so much, my sweetheart. Please, come closer to me. I need to feel your touch."

The butterfly descended, touching my left elbow and flying toward the stairs to the basement. I of course followed it and saw it at the steps, but right as I got down into the basement and looked everywhere, it was gone!

January 13, 2013—not exactly a butterfly season, and that butterfly shook my whole existence and changed my views and beliefs! I, who was trained as a scientist, started seeing things differently and pondering some questions that previously had always had reasonable scientific explanations but not any longer. I do believe that I was privileged to get a glimpse into the other reality. It sounds surreal, but it really happened!

When I told others about this, people would tell me that I was probably stressed too much and that sometimes causes delusions, or maybe it was a medication side effect (I was prescribed antidepressants and benzodiazepines but was not taking any). All I knew was that it was real!

I became very selective about whom I told my butterfly story to. I debated for a long time whether it should be in this book, but then I decided that my story would be incomplete, untold, if I left out this chapter.

As I said, it shook me to the core and changed me and my beliefs! Just a month or two later, I was struggling and upset again—sad, unsure—and my flickering visitor appeared again! As I was in the kitchen, bent over the counter and holding my head, I felt motion on the left side of my face! It was a butterfly and before I even said anything, it disappeared! I know it sounds crazy, unbelievable, and the reader has an option to believe it or not, but it happened...

My children of course know my story, but even they brushed it off as unbelievable until one day life threw them for a loop. That is a story for another chapter.

I have my butterfly on Isaak's memorial stone. I see some readers smirk or altogether brush it off. That is all right. Everything has a purpose, time, and place. Like I said, I am actually very selective who I tell my butterfly story to. But it is mine, and it is a very important and precious story that completes me!

Obviously in summer I see a lot of butterflies, and whenever I stop, they linger and stay on the flowers, plants, even come and sit on my hand. People would say that it's summer and there are many butterflies around... Maybe...

But the one I saw on January 13, 2013? I love that butterfly forever, just like I love Isaak forever. I do believe that his soul turned into the butterfly and that is how he continues to watch over us!

My house is a shrine to the butterfly! Decorations, posters, pillows, earrings. And I always look for live ones, and they come and are always with me. So many butterfly stories... They warm my heart and penetrate my soul!

21

A NEW MEANING OF *DEPRESSION*

PEOPLE OFTEN SAY THAT TIME HEALS, AND IT OFTEN DOES, BUT ONLY TO a certain extent and in different ways in different people. In 2013 I found myself completely enveloped in grief and depression.

Grief has been studied for centuries by so many scientists, and it still not well understood. Simply because we all grieve in our own way. Probably the worst that you could say to a grieving person is that you understand their grief?! Really everyone grieves in their own way.

Leo Tolstoy in the novel *Anna Karenina* said: "Happy families are all alike; every unhappy family is unhappy in its own way." Same with grief—we all grieve in our own way.

The wound in my heart was so deep and so unbearable that even though I started to get out of my "shell," it was still unending winter and cold in my heart.

The wound of loss was so profound and deep, and yes, it would heal with time. As a medical person, I would call it a secondary healing. It's a term that is most commonly used for a wound healing that got complicated by an untoward event (most commonly an infection). That type of healing usually leaves an ugly scar after prolonged healing. That is what translates to an ugly emotional scar in your heart when you lose the love of your life.

Even though I had to get out and do things that I had never done before (as Isaak was always doing them), those first four years were really in a fog for me. I could've had Denzel Washington or George Clooney walk by me and I would not have seen them!

There were daily tasks that needed to be taken care of, and I had to do my best, because anything other than my best would not be Isaak's way of doing it.

The first time I came with my taxes to the CPA and cried in his office, he advised that I actually had done a good job on prepping all the needed documents and calculations, etc. On time! Isaak never delayed even once, and I needed to do that in his memory. Then our CPA told me that initially he had not liked Isaak much, as Isaak would always find a mistake or show how it could be done differently. But then the CPA added that even though Isaak was a stickler for numbers, he later "grew on me." Yes, Isaak was always good with numbers and was smart. I was proud that I was able to do a decent job in his memory (and numbers are not my strong point)!

The majority of the tasks were unpleasant, bureaucratic, and frequently difficult. As much as people would say that they were very sorry about my loss and so on, they would require that I go on a mission of scanning and faxing his death certificate, and some—even after all of that—just didn't get it. You see such an incredible misunderstanding in efficiency and no sensitivity. I have to admit that I was not able to change some accounts and just left his name there!

Maybe people were trying to do their jobs, but for me it was stabbing in my deep heart wound every time I had to fax that death certificate! I had to live through that and walk that dark tunnel hoping that there would be a spark of light at the end.

And there was an incidental, totally unexpected therapy for my grief that I simply discovered not in a psychiatrist's or psychologist's office but at the AAA office. I had to exchange the AAA card to be in my name, and I was in line in the office in Beaverton holding the AAA card in Isaak's name and his death certificate. While I was in line, I saw this beautiful picture of some tropical paradise on the wall. At that moment, I felt that that was what I needed to do. I needed to get away from myself!

I was doing it every day going on a different walks, but this idea was on a much bigger scale and that was my therapy! The idea was born, and for the first time in three months, I was looking toward something and felt anxious and excited. Maybe a small light was coming into my vision and my heart!

22

TRAVEL BECAME MY SAVIOR

So, I was in that AAA line, and when my turn came, I took care of changing the name on the card, and then I asked if they had a travel agent available, and they said that they did. I waited for the agent now. I was thinking, *I am retired now, and both physically and financially I am doing okay. Why not travel freestyle and really get away without a deadline of returning to work or taking care of other business and family? Yes, that is truly "going away from myself"!!!! I am doing it!*

In about five to seven minutes, I was taken to the office in the back and met Bonnie, a cheerful young lady who sounded like she could do anything. I did not take cheer easily in those days, but somehow I was at ease with Bonnie. I gave her a rather long and not very cheerful explanation of my situation and told her that I needed to get away, preferably for a long time.

That would be the first time that I would be traveling alone, and Alone is a very lonely state, but looking back, I feel that if I had not done it, then I might not be writing these pages now!

I also had my beautiful memories to hold on to so close to my wounded heart! Luckily, Isaak and I had traveled together a lot, and I am so glad that we did not wait for retirement... We were both full-time professionals, but nevertheless we took some beautiful and long vacations, and we were fortunate and happy to be able to visit five continents and so many amazing places and different cultures. You could say that we were both "travel hungry" and both loved exploring new places, meeting different people. While in the Soviet Union, we could not even dream about going out of the country. Borders were very tight and the system was too bureaucratic to go anywhere.

So after talking to Bonnie for another twenty to thirty minutes, I was (without realizing it) making monumental plans for myself. I had visited five continents with Isaak, and I decided that I needed to see the other two continents: Antarctica and Africa. There was unfinished business with Machu Picchu (where Isaak and I had been set to go but had to cancel at the last minute, as elevation and bad lungs do not agree). And of course the Galápagos Islands were in that general area.

Bonnie and I started working out details for that great voyage. I decided that I would go to Antarctica, and I remember throwing away a "special deal" brochure, but of course Bonnie had an even better deal in her pocket. I had done a cruise with Isaak before for seven or ten days. Bonnie showed me a twenty-one-day Holland America cruise, and looking back, I am so glad that I chose that instead of the thirteen days on Princess Cruises.

The reason being that both cruises would circle South America, but the Holland branched out from Ushuaia to spend eight days in the Antarctic Peninsula.

Everything about that time in the Antarctic Peninsula—from how they prepared before entrance by removing all the ashtrays and food from the decks to the amazing scenery—truly was a dream! That pristine, extremely white, and isolated place was very cold but definitely a dreamy place. Definitely one of a kind! Seeing huge icebergs floating by, hundreds if not thousands of penguins swimming very fast, and untouched nature was a big, white, cold but amazing dream. Some people say that there's not too much to see in Antarctica, but to me it was so beautiful. I liked the isolation at that time, as it fit my isolated soul. Also, the captain was very knowledgeable and careful. He announced three or four times that the plan was to go into Paradise Bay, but then he felt that it was not safe to do it so we never entered the cove. I also did not understand why my camera quit on me so often, and I kept running to my room to recharge it. Apparently extreme cold drains your camera batteries?

The rest of the cruise circling the tip of South America, we also had amazing scenery, especially in Patagonia and Tierra del Fuego. Except Antarctica's pristine nature is like nothing else in the world! And I love penguins, and I've seen so many of different kinds!

Socializing, dinners were so hard for me. I was as isolated as Antarctica. I had no communication with my children. No phone, no iPad. My daughter was very unhappy that I'd left without any way of communication, to which I told her in my very depressed manner that if the plane fell out of the sky, she would hear about it in the news. If our ship hit an iceberg and sank, she would also hear about it. I was sure of that. Needless to say that she was unhappy about my reasoning, but I left without the phone anyway!

When I would come to the dining room, the staff would always try to put me at a bigger table so I would be able to socialize with other people, but it absolutely did not work for me. I asked for a table for two and wanted to dine by myself. Then I finally got a small table for two, and it was just for me. I did not have to pretend or make small conversation and start crying. It was my first dinner by myself, and I did not think of what to order. The main menu had all meat dishes (and I did not eat meat at the time), so I ordered a grilled salmon from everyday dishes. They brought me a beautiful dish of grilled salmon with mashed potato and asparagus.

That was exactly what Isaak had for his first meal after surgery before the nasty adenovirus got hold of his new lungs and claimed his life! It took away forever the love of my life, my sweet husband, Isaak! As I told you previously, the nurse who watched him clear the plate said that she had no doubt that he would leave the ICU in six weeks. Unfortunately, he did not!!! When I saw my plate, my memories enveloped me, and I started crying very bitterly. Half of the kitchen and dining room staff gathered around me and asked what was wrong. How could I explain it? I just left the dining room!

The next day I got an invitation from the director of guest services and public relations to come in and talk. I did, and I cried and told her the story, and she understood (as she had just recently lost her mother), and she insisted I call my daughter right from her office. I did talk to my daughter twice and reassured her that everything was okay. For Valentine's Day, the office sent me nice flowers. I did befriend a nice lady from Canada also traveling by herself, as she'd recently lost her significant other. We met on a top deck while watching wildlife together, and we continued to meet and do that together. But then we each had our space and were not interested in attending other functions. We were alone with our respective griefs.

From Antarctica I toured South America some more (Valparaíso and Santiago, Chile). Then we got to the mysterious Machu Picchu and hiked to the highest point, Sun Gate. What an incredible place that was. Seismologists and engineers come to Machu Picchu to try to understand how those structures are still standing after centuries, and no mortar was used in the construction. It's really mindboggling. And the culture is beautiful with very friendly people and delicious pisco sour drinks. I ate more blue corn there than I have in my whole life! Altitude sickness got me a bit in Cusco, but coca tea saved the day. In a hotel in Cusco, that's what they greet you with for refreshments, and I stayed in the hotel lobby drinking it until nighttime!

The following year (2014), I traveled to Africa! What an amazing continent with beautiful, proud, and hardworking people. Going on a safari was an unforgettable experience. When you are in an open Jeep and a herd of elephants crosses five feet from you, a giraffe eats leaves from the tree three to five feet from you, an elephant swims and plays in the water, a leopard stretches in the tree just above your head, and then you see birds and animals you did not know existed, it does not take much to fall in love with Africa! People are very proud. We were in some very poor areas, but there was not a single beggar. They tried to sell things, but there was absolutely no begging. In Botswana, it was amazing to see road signs everywhere for honey for sale. Cape Town, South Africa, with Table Mountain and Victoria Falls in Zimbabwe had the most beautiful rainbows all over and are such unforgettable and gorgeous sites! I just went there for a continent and came back with a love for the continent and its people!

Now I'd completed my continents and then was traveling more and more. I would be gone more than I would be at home. It was incredible to see the world!

I got to North Cape, Iceland, and climbed the Pulpit Rock in Norway (an absolute dream), then went through Norwegian fjords, Turkey, Poland, Germany, Czech Republic, Hungary, Croatia, back to Australia and New Zealand, Easter Island, Japan, and then just in 2019 Italy, France, and Spain. I also visited the amazing Galápagos Islands. I could write a separate book about all my travels. I do want to tell you about Easter Island and the mysterious moai monolithic statue giants!

So, I saw that little dot in the middle of the map of the Pacific Ocean and read about the statues, and I needed to get there! Princess Cruises were celebrating their fiftieth anniversary, and it was a twenty-five-day cruise to Easter Island and Pacific islands of Moorea and Tahiti. The price was unbelievable, and I found a lady in one of the widow support groups who loved cruising, and we decided to go together for twenty-five days?! (We are still good friends!) This would be the first time we traveled together, and neither one of us had done a cruise for that long. So, there we were with beautiful scenery, on a smaller ship, and a day before we were supposed to land on Easter Island, our captain told us at dinner that he had sailed that route five times and only once stopped at Easter Island??? You see, that small island was formed by a volcanic eruption a long time ago, and when lava spilled, it formed really large rocks all around the island, and if it was stormy (and it often is) and the waves reached thirty feet, it's unsafe to land in small boats (tender boats) like ours. We would know tomorrow as we approached the island. According to the captain, the chances were really small to land on the island. My friend and I had purchased a full tour through the island, and I really wanted to see it!

The next morning, I was on the upper deck so I would not miss the chance to at least get a quick glance at the moai statues, as they are seen on approach like they are guarding the island. I was talking to my sweet Isaak and telling him how much I wanted to get there! It just so happened that a professional photographer happened to be standing behind me! The captain announced that it looked like we wouldn't be able to land on the island because the waves were too high for tender boats, etc. I looked at the horizon, and at that very time, a most beautiful rainbow rolled like a red carpet over the ocean and straight to our ship. At that moment I knew that we would land on Easter Island! The photographer behind me exclaimed that he had never seen a rainbow do that and was clicking away pictures. I caught one too. I turned around and said: "Yes, you would not, but this is a special rainbow!" It was my entrance to Easter Island! It's a mysterious and not well understood piece of history how those statues were made or how they got to the island. Even more mysterious—but understood by me—is how we landed there, three hours later, but we did!! Life began to return into my emotionally lifeless body! I was not healed, but I was on the way to recovery!

I want to share something else at the end of this chapter. When Isaak passed away, I was distraught, broken, and lost. Painfully sad. Isaak's nurse came up to me and asked if I wanted a fingerprint or a lock of hair from Isaak. I did not comprehend what she was saying or, for that matter, what anybody was saying. Isaak did have a head of beautiful hair that I believe that our daughter inherited. Anyway I ended up with a pouch of his hair. Every place I go, I deposit a small strand of it.

So, my love, your DNA has gone to Antarctica, Africa, and many other places! You, Isaak, continue to travel with me—we've gone to all the continents together. You, Isaak, will live forever in my heart, and the hearts of our children and grandchildren! This is a short story of how travel really saved me and put me on the way to recovery! It was happy, sad, funny, exciting, scary at times, with plain stupid moments, but it was great and healing medicine for my broken HEART!

23

DAY AT THE MUSEUM—
SUMMER 2014

IT WAS THE SUMMER OF 2014, AND THE PORTLAND ART MUSEUM HAD A
special Parisian show. There were exhibits inside and outside
with fun fare in the Park Blocks with entertainers and performers. It was a beautiful summer day, and I was meeting a few
friends and planning to spend all day at the museum. I frequently
do, as I like to take my time and look at art, read about it, etc.
So, here I was at the museum, meeting my friends. We looked
at the beautiful Eiffel Tower in the main exhibit, then had food
and enjoyed music and dancer acrobats in the Park Blocks. The
sculpture garden outside was incredible. We spent two to three
hours outside, and then my friends decided that they were done,
but of course, I returned back to the museum.

You see, I'd seen the main exhibit and all other halls upstairs
and in the modern art building, but I didn't get to the basement

where frequently they have photo exhibits. I always love to check it out when I go to the museum. I love photo exhibits! I went to the basement, and before entering the hall, I saw a large glass case with a big open book, which gave an explanation about the exhibit. It was an exhibit of an apparently famous photographer by the name of Garry Winogrand who in the 1960s or 1970s took pictures of women by candid camera (such as in phone booths, at street cafés, in buildings, etc.). The name of his book is *Women Are Beautiful*.

As he explained in the book, he was not looking for outside beauty but more for expression, body language, outer beauty of expression, attitude, so to say for their "inner beauty." The main photos from his book are part of the permanent exhibit in the Metropolitan Museum of Art in New York. He had thousands of pictures on film that had not been developed, as Garry died suddenly at the age of fifty-six on March 19, 1984. He left behind a lot of unprocessed work. There were more then 300,000 unedited images. One critic said that the inner beauty of the women in the book shined through their pose expressions. Women in *Women Are Beautiful* are vibrant, happy, self-confident, and uninhibited. They carved their own path and followed without intimidation and embraced their freedom to take on the eras despite what others may say! I knew very little about Garry Winogrand or his work, but now I was very excited to see his work!

To see the photos I went to the exhibit hall, and it just so happened that I was the only one in the exhibit at that time. I entered and started on the wall on the right side. Suddenly in the middle of that wall, I saw a picture simply titled "Untitled (Cafe,

Paris, France)," taken in 1969. In the photo there are two women in a café in Paris having coffee. One is looking at the camera, and she is in a white outfit and smiling, and another one is looking down into her purse looking for something.

But in the instant that I saw that young lady, I wanted to scream and shout at the top of my lungs, "It's me!!!!"

But in 1969 I was just finishing high school and was never in Paris. That image consumed me completely! As I said previously in 1969 I was in Ukraine and could not have been in a Parisian café?! But the woman in the picture was me!!! A mirror image of me. If I'd had a twin sister, we could not look more alike! She looked maybe twenty-five in that photo. As I said, I could not see her eyes, but her face, hair, mouth (rather small like my father's was) were matches. Even her long fingers holding the cigarette—although I never smoked...

The whole five minutes shook me to the core! I could not even finish looking at the other photographs. I went home, and in spite of my poor technical computer skills, I dove into computer search. I needed to find that woman. I needed to learn more about Garry Winogrand, the photographer, and maybe, just maybe, find the link to the mysterious woman in that photograph?

I really do not know how I did it without help (and on the first try), but I located the book and even was able to print out the photograph (that is big for me!). I completely became obsessed with the mystery woman in the photograph! I reached out to a distant cousin and shared the story and picture with him. He was a family tree geek and always was finding people related to us. I asked him if he could find people who worked with Garry Winogrand or were close to him and maybe give me an idea of how to find the woman in that photograph. He did an extensive search, but a lot of leads were dead-ends.

He did find Mr. Winogrand's son, who lived in the San Francisco area and I guess has the rights to the undeveloped photos but had little interest in his father's work, and of course at the time all the pictures were taken spontaneously without any informed consent forms signed. So there really was no way to track down who that mysterious twin of mine was in that photo.

I was so affected by that encounter that I decided to email my brother just the picture without telling the story. At that point, he was the only person left who knew me at that age. He told me later that as he was looking at the picture in my email, his wife, Dina, walked by, saw the photo, and said, "What is Raisa's picture doing in your email?" She knew me young, and she immediately asked that. When I called my brother and asked him if he recognized anybody in the photo, he told me: "Of course, it was you in the black coat."

Then I told my brother the whole story about the museum, the date on photo, and the fact that it was taken in Paris, where we'd never been at that time, etc. I told him how puzzled and stunned I was by the whole experience. My brother simply replied: "Remember that our father was captured in Czechoslovakia, and then when he escaped, he was sheltered by that nice family and spent some time recuperating in that small village?"

As I mentioned previously, we were born after the war, but grew up with stories of war, songs, and music from the time. Dad spoke very tenderly about the family who sheltered him, spoke of them with love! And always said that they treated him as their own son. We were small kids, not at all interested in details, stories. We loved our musical hours, but even then, we felt love coming from what he was telling—even as kids, we sensed it. We thought that it was a gratitude for saving his life, but it could've been much more...I'm not even sure if he ever mentioned their names or even if he remembered them himself.

My father was a single soldier from the Soviet Army, twenty-eight years old in 1944, and it is very possible that the family had a daughter of that age... Times were terrible, but people were still falling in love? I might've had a sister, but I will never know??? I'm not sure that my father even knew or suspected??? Another life secret, potentially uncovered but never told! And now there is no one to ask any longer!

I keep repeating it again and again: please ask your family questions. No matter how boring or unimportant the details might seem at the time. They just might become vitally important later in life! That is the big reason for this book!

24

SUNRIVER, OREGON, HOLIDAY TO REMEMBER! 2015–2016

Both my daughter's and my birthdays are in August. For a few years we decided to make it a tradition to get away to some fun places and simply have fun! So, a few years in a row we loved going to Sunriver for a week or two. In 2014, we did that and stayed at a home with bicycles (of course, biking is one of the main recreational activities).

My daughter's family is full of good bikers. I rediscovered biking that summer after probably a forty-year hiatus. We biked all together by the river, a lot around the town, on trails, to the pool, etc. We just had an incredible summer and decided to make it an annual tradition to do that and return to Sunriver! My grandkids (who were teenagers now) were also excited, and each one wanted to bring a friend the next year. So, it was all decided, and I began to consider buying a bicycle for my home and riding it on my trail by the river!

On a completely unrelated issue, I also have a fear of heights, and that next year, August of 2015, I decided to conquer it. On the day when everybody was arriving in Portland from Seattle—a beautiful warm day in August—I went to Newberg and flew in a hot air balloon. It was the most amazing experience, and I ended up having an incredible day. When I drove back, I thought, *Life is good! I feel lonely at times, but I just conquered my fear of heights, and I am over sixty and have not had a single surgery!*

The next day, all together with my daughter's family and both grandkids' friends, we headed to Sunriver for another awesome vacation! I was very excited and looking forward to fun times with the family and especially to riding a bicycle again! We all went to town, then to the pool, on our bikes and spent essentially all day on bikes after we arrived.

The next morning we decided to do my favorite, the River Loop. After breakfast we all started riding, and my son-in-law, Chad (who was a very good biker), and all four kids were in front, and my daughter, Lilya, and I were in the back. She was behind me. As we were approaching a small slope and going down, I saw that coming toward me were three bicyclists who took up the whole small trail, and if I continued, I would ride into them! So, I veered off to the left, next to the riverbank, and I ended on a patch of small pebbles and lost my balance and fell off the bike. The heavy bike landed right on top of my right ankle and crushed it into many small pieces. I knew instantly that I had a bad fracture (break), as my foot was completely on the ground and angled to the right.

The nicest lady stopped and offered her phone to call 911. She looked at my foot and its strange positioning and naively asked why my right foot looked so different, to which I replied, "That's because it is broken." My daughter, who was right behind me, was not able to even look at it. She immediately called her husband, and he was back with the kids. He did some manipulation (luckily Chad is an ER doctor), and then I was taken by ambulance to the ER in Bend. I had surgery that day, and in a week my son, David, picked me up and brought me home. I had a cast and in six weeks should've been healed and fine with rehabilitation. I guess it was not meant to be, and the nightmare started!

I had an appointment with a local orthopedist (who shall remain unnamed) in two weeks. In one week, I started feeling worse—fever, nausea, vomiting, loss of appetite, fatigue, and chills. Enough symptoms for any layperson to know it was an infection. At that point I did not think that I was able to wait for another week, and I started feverishly (literally and figuratively speaking) trying to get in sooner. In that condition I was trying to fight the system to be seen sooner, and as a health care provider I was trying to avoid an "unnecessary" ER visit! It was very necessary, though, as my fever was very high, even with all the ibuprofen and Tylenol I was taking! I should've gone to ER then... After two frustrating days on the phone in what I believe was a preseptic condition, I still did not have an appointment, but I told my son to drive me to the office and if they wouldn't see me, to take me to the ER. He took me to the office, and on the way there, I got a call that they would see me.

I was in the waiting room very sick, throwing up, fever of 104 degrees, chills, and then when I saw the orthopedist and my cast was removed, I could see erythema (redness around my stitches). I politely asked if he would put me on antibiotics and he replied, "NO." Anybody—and I mean anybody—should've seen the evidence of a post-op infection that was screaming in his face, but I guess he did not! Yes, we are all human and make mistakes, but thinking back I just cannot help thinking that maybe, just maybe, I could've avoided the year of hell that ensued! Instead, the orthopedist sent me to see a primary care doctor to evaluate why I had a fever and slopped on a new hot cast to help "cook" up my infection and send me home.

I won't describe everything in the absolute and total nightmare that I lived for the next ten months! In short, at another ER visit the next week, my cast was removed, and again other things were pursued instead of looking at the obvious, and finally when I pointed to it, the doctor said that I would be hospitalized as soon as a bed became available. It was a total disaster during hospitalization—three more surgeries, a CV line for antibiotics that were administered four times a day for eight weeks, bleeding out of the wound, becoming anemic, one month at a nursing home thinking that I was going to lose my mind, endless useless appointments with an orthopedic and plastic surgeon, home health visits, and so on. Not getting anywhere. I could probably write a whole book on that. As I said, we are all human and make mistakes, but I honestly feel embarrassed and sad for my medical profession that unfortunately as a patient I ended up experiencing one mistake after another. I lost a year of my life paying for those mistakes!

Finally, I self-referred to the wound clinic and a doctor I knew from my work, and I begged, "Please help." He was terrified too, but after twelve weeks of treatment (including some experimental treatments), I was determined to be healed—with a very ugly scar on my right ankle but healed nevertheless!!!! I was so scarred and sore that taking a normal shower without protecting my wound was almost impossible. Yes, the scar was ugly.

The end of 2015 and most of 2016 remain a horrible nightmare in my mind, but I am here and I am alive and I am able to walk! And I am an ultimate optimist, and there was very little during that time to be optimistic about, but at that nursing home (where I was losing my mind and my health), I looked online at DreamTrips (just to travel virtually and get my mind off everything). I saw Pulpit Rock in Norway as number one on the site's list, and it was love at first sight. At that time, when I was not able to walk and did not know if I would ever walk again, I decided that I needed to climb Pulpit Rock, and it's a miracle of life that I did climb it successfully in 2017!

25

MEETING CALE

It was a beautiful day in April 2016. I was walking on my usual trail along the waterfront near my home. I was still wearing an orthopedic shoe on my right foot and was desperately trying to recover from the nightmare that I had been living since August 2015.

As I was walking on this trail, lost in thought about my recovery and wound care, suddenly a man smiled and said hello. Just like a scene from a movie—he had me at hello. I know it sounds crazy, but it was like someone touched me on the shoulder and said, "Look!" And then I saw him! He was tall and slender with blondish-gray hair and dark sunglasses. Boy, I sure hate sunglasses—I needed to see his eyes!!! But most reasonable people do wear sunglasses when it's sunny. Then I thought, *He's just a friendly person that said hi.* But I caught myself thinking about seeing him again on a future walk.

For some reason, I started looking for him on the trail, and we ended up passing by each other daily. And it was always a short hello, dark glasses (even on cloudy days), and off he'd go. This went on for about six or seven months, until one day our conversation became a touch longer—like two sentences longer. He began to talk to me about different routes to take on the trails and which restaurants he enjoyed visiting. And then eloquently he would say, "I need to go now." Later I realized that even though we'd spoken a few times, I didn't even know his name.

Finally, one day I built up the courage to ask him his name. So, we introduced ourselves and he began to open up even more, telling me he'd recently moved up here from California (just like everyone else in Portland). Also, coincidentally, he lived two buildings away from my house, which explained why we so frequently bumped into each other.

When I asked him what brought him to Portland, he replied that he wasn't at liberty to discuss it yet! I have a very vivid imagination, or maybe I watch a little too much of investigative dramas on television, but between him avoiding questions and leaving so soon and wearing dark sunglasses...my mind went nuts running a whole slew of possibilities—that he was running away from someone or something, hiding something really serious behind those dark glasses, etc., etc.

And then one day I asked him to take off the sunglasses so I could see his eyes. He obliged and revealed beautiful blue eyes with an eerie soullessness about them. I essentially didn't even see any pupils!!!

So, as usual, I was on my trail taking walks by the river and thinking of my mystery man. All I knew was that his name was Cale. (And the first time I heard it, I blurted out some nonsense, "You mean like that lettuce?" He politely replied, "Yes, except with a *C*.") My soulless stranger.

Mystery enveloped me and penetrated deep to my bones like a cold winter. The web of my curiosity became so intricate, I became more and more determined to find out what was hiding behind those dark glasses of this polite, soft-spoken, and soulless man. *Who is this stranger? Why do I want to know more about him? I still don't know why he moved to Portland from California.*

My benign attempts to stop him and have a conversation continued to fail repeatedly. For example, I bombarded him, "Not many people move from sun to rain. It must be for work. It must be for family." His polite response was "I am used to the rain. I grew up in Seattle." I noticed a wedding ring and asked if he was married. Another polite response: "I was for four years but no longer." His ability to predict things was almost scary. On one of our quick encounters, he predicted my future. I mentioned an upcoming trip to Australia to celebrate the New Year. I was looking forward to going through Milford Sound, which is a beautiful passage, a gorge that would have likely been the highlight of my trip. It was canceled. As he predicted, my ship never made it, as it was too stormy and too dangerous to traverse.

On another beautiful and bright morning on the trail, as I walked with a friend, there he was. The presence of my friend filled me with bravery, and I asked for Cale's number. Upon the exchange of numbers, I also asked for a date. I invited him to the Portland Winter Light Festival near OMSI. I had previously set myself up to go with friends. I felt bad to cancel on them, but I needed to get Cale alone and maybe uncover the mystery.

It was January 31, 2017, and it felt like the coldest day of the year. We made plans to walk to OMSI over the Tillicum Crossing Bridge. I was so excited to have Cale to myself. *What mystery from his past might unfold?* I was like a teenager full of anticipation!

At exactly 5:00 p.m., as agreed, he rang my doorbell (and what felt like all my other bells). He was all bundled up, and it was endearing how he said to make sure that I put on my hat because it was very cold and heat is mainly lost through the head. I didn't want to wear a hat—I never wear hats—but on that night I did.

On our walk we made small talk about the program for the light show, the sternwheeler ride, and the opera performers. When we were in the middle of the new bridge, all illuminated and gorgeous, he slowed down and told me rather casually and matter-of-factly, "I have a glioblastoma, brain cancer, stage four, and I was given seventeen months to live, which is almost up. Shortly after my diagnosis and prognosis, I sold my home and my business in Los Angeles, gave away most of my possessions to friends (not having any family), and moved to Portland to get a 'right to die,' which wasn't available in California at the time. They just passed the law in California this month, and I will be returning to California in three to four weeks. It's good that you stopped me on the trail because I'm moving away soon. I have a friend in Rancho Mirage who has offered to let me stay in a guesthouse."

His mystery unfolded quickly as he dropped one bomb after another. Before I knew it, our walk was over and we were boarding the sternwheeler at the light show.

As our night continued, I was truly amazed at how casual, friendly, and funny he was as he socialized with other people. There was not a drop of bitterness or fear in this man with essentially a death sentence. On the sternwheeler, the talent of the opera singers consumed the air, but I could only hear Cale. He continued with his story. He had been diagnosed in October of 2015 after suffering seizures. He was forced to stop driving and sell his business. He refused surgery and was now on some kind of experimental medicine from Oregon Health & Science University (OHSU) is a hospital that is right on our trail. And the reason we continued to cross paths.

As we walked home, he pointed out an apartment he almost rented. It was off our trail. We would have never met. His story continued to unfold. One more bitter turn on our bitterly cold night. He had been born premature and was abused from a very young age. In the sixties people didn't talk about abuse and violence. He sought help from churches, teachers, and even his grandparents. They were all dismissive of his pleas, writing them off as lies and fantasies. He ran away from home at the age of seven. He jumped trains, landing himself in juvenile detention (riding a train without a ticket is a federal offense), and then he was handed back over to his abusers. At age eleven he ran away again. Another visit to juvenile detention, and he was put into foster care and then adopted by a family in Seattle. He became good friends with his adoptive mother. Years later his adopted siblings wrongfully blamed him for their parents' divorce.

As I listened to his story, I felt awfully sad for his lost childhood, the lack of love in his life, and then his tragic diagnosis. Everything inside of me wanted to do something nice for this man, no matter how small, that would show him he was loved. I told him that he was worthy of love. After this date he told me many times how glad he was that I stopped him on that trail.

Cale moved back to Rancho Mirage a few short weeks after our evening together. He beat the cancer and was cancer-free for a whole year. I visited him in Palm Springs during that year, rejoicing in his cancer-free life. Cale came to visit me in Portland in 2020—it felt like a final formal goodbye, as his cancer had returned and he was bravely fighting. He is now being treated for two types of cancer. We continue to stay in contact via phone and the occasional exchange of cards and written letters. A man who admitted to never loving anybody tells me freely now "I love you." And it is nothing intimate, but it feels good to give that nice but very unfortunate man a glimpse of the brightness of love (whether it is motherly, sisterly, or friendly)!

26

MICHAEL AND ANNE

I'VE EXPERIENCED GRIEF IN MY LIFE BUT ALSO WAS AND AM BLESSED, AND I count my blessings every day! God did bless Isaak and me with two wonderful children, who then in turn blessed us again with my dearest and incredibly, deeply loved grandkids.

So, in the early 2000s our first grandson, Michael, blessed us with his arrival. Born in Texas with a somewhat complicated initial arrival into this world, he made us grandparents. We were very proud of our new title! Michael was named for my father, the man with the big heart, a loving and caring man, and Michael would definitely grow up carrying those wonderful traits!

Michael grew up a very smart, cautious child. From a very young age, he became interested in trivia (such as Ripley's Believe It or Not!) and memorized lots of facts—different sports facts, names of teams, player statistics, coaches, etc. He seemed to have a brain and memory that would just soak up all that information and store it, probably as young as age seven or eight. He was also good at playing many different sports—soccer, basketball, baseball—and we could not be more proud of our grandson as we watched him play all of those! He would constantly learn not only the game but also different sports trivia and all about different sports teams and players (including some very difficult names that we could not even pronounce), their achievements, etc. He was pretty much a walking encyclopedia of different facts. At a very young age, he started playing fantasy football with his grandpa Al and uncle Matthew and winning at times! He just had an incredible memory, and we both were very proud of him. His grandpa Isaak was so incredibly proud of him (even though Grandpa did not know half of those facts or names). And of course, there is a funny story about that!

It was one of the spring breaks in school, and Michael had just turned seven or eight and his sister, Anne, was almost six. We were all in Hawaii. We were at our hotel pool—I was in the water playing a shark game with the kids, and Isaak was poolside under an umbrella with a couple of men who seemed to be in a heated discussion about something. I was not sure what, but I came out of the pool for a few minutes of a break and just to say hi and see how Isaak was doing. At that point Isaak told those guys that his grandson would come out of the pool and tell them exactly what and who and when. Those two gentleman waved dismissively at Isaak, almost as if saying: "Yes, right." Just kind of saying that they understood how grandparents are proud of their grandkids, but what would an eight-year-old know about that? I was not clued in on the topic of their discussion/dispute, but all I knew was that the men were from Pittsburg.

When I went back to the pool, I told Michael that "D" (his name for Grandpa Isaak) might need his help in some sports discussion. Michael stepped out of the pool, came up to Isaak and those two guys, and after listening to their discussion for a minute or two, he simply said that Pittsburg's hockey team is the Penguins and the best player is such-and-such, and in the game that they were discussing, he did this and that and scored that much. I will never forget how those guys looked at our Michael in total amazement! When they'd waved and dismissed Isaak, saying, oh yes, all grandparents think that their grandkids are the most amazing and most smart, they sure were in for a surprise!!! The last thing that they expected was some seven- or eight-year-old from Seattle to settle their dispute almost effortlessly!

Our sweet granddaughter, Anne, was also born in Texas. She was named for my mom, Anna, and her middle name, Katheryn, is for my matriarch Grandma Khasya (who helped me when my daughter was born). She sure was named for two strong, smart women in our family and the best cooks! I wonder if she will inherit the cooking traits?

That sweet child, from a very young age, has shown a love for art, drawing, and colors. She loves kids, and from a very young age was a babysitter for the neighbor's kids (just like her mom). She was really good at different sports, anything from gymnastics to cheerleading to soccer to softball to basketball, track and field, and dancing. She was good in all of those. Her grandpa Isaak was very proud of her artwork, and even when he was very ill in the ICU at UW and was transferred to a different room, he asked me to make sure that ALL of Annie's artwork was transferred with him. That was his most cherished possession!

Like I said Anne was good in many sports, but cheerleading was the one that made me extremely nervous! When we watched those cheerleading competitions, my heart would often skip a beat when she was thrown in the air, and I would pray for her to land right or to be caught on time. For a few years, she was so into cheerleading, and she was cartwheeling, taking huge leaps in the air, and she did it anywhere we would go, on the sidewalks, on the cement floor, anywhere. That made me so very nervous! Annie, you've always made me so proud over the years, and I love you so very much! You are a beautiful person both in and out, and I know that no matter where life will take you, we will always be proud of you! You are a true gift!

Now I would like to conclude this chapter with another cute story, where both of my sweet grandkids are the major players.

Michael was not quite eleven yet, and Anne is almost eight and a half. I was watching them while their parents were in China on a vacation. One day after school, Michael told me that he needed to go to the neighborhood across the highway. He would go on a bike. He was not sure exactly where the playground was, but he was going to find it and meet a friend. I saw those cheeks glowing in pinkish color of excitement and his sparkling eyes of anticipation! *OMG! My baby is having his first date!* I was now as excited as he probably was, but I told him that with all my love for him, I could not allow him to cross the highway on a bicycle by himself (and it's a busy road like most of them in Seattle and vicinity). I said that we would go together, and my car would be next to his bike, and after we found the playground, I would be as inconspicuous as possible and not interfere or even pretend to know him. I would be in the distance. He worried about Anne interfering, "as she usually does," and I promised to keep her with me. After a few failed attempts to talk me out of going with him, we were on our way.

So, we were heading to the neighborhood across the highway. It was rush hour, and we were lined up behind many cars. I was rolling very slowly, and Michael was on his bike trying to talk to Anne in the backseat. He was begging her not to shadow him on the playground. There were many cars behind me—everyone was going very slow, but I was probably the slowest. All of the sudden, a car behind me flashed its lights, stopped, and a lady from that car came to my window. Michael was once again using the moment that we stopped and having a heated discussion with Anne and asking her again and again not to tailgate him at the playground.

The lady from the car behind looked at me and then asked Michael if anybody was harassing him. He said that I am his grandma and everything is okay. That vigilant lady warmed my heart even though I was a suspect. We need more people like her who care enough to stop her car and figure out what is going on. We finally turned, but Michael did not know where the playground was. So he knocked at the first door in this neighborhood, and they gave him directions. We arrived on the playground, and I asked Anne to stay with me, but of course she wanted to go on the swings. Michael knew it and that she would follow him!

I sat on the furthest bench from where Michael was. Christina (the date) was not there yet, so my Michael went straight to the blackberry bushes and start picking and eating them intensely. Anne was off the swings and next to Michael doing the same.

Then I saw a beautiful blond girl come into the playground. She was all dressed up. A vision of light and brightness in a light-green skirt and a white sheer blouse. My sweet Michael turned around from the bushes to face her and OMG! His face was all smeared with blackberries. I made a faint attempt to gesture to him to wipe his face, but he could not see that. Anne was next to him like a bee on honey. Christina had come to the playground with a teenage girl, probably her older sister, who had similar blondish hair. She also sat on the furthest bench, essentially across from me. She was looking at them and smiling! At this point, there was not much I could do about Anne. So, all three of them talked and played on the playground! It was seven or eight years ago, and I remember it like it was yesterday! That sweet young love! Ahh.

The most memorable thing. I took my Michael to his first date! And I was powerless to stop his sweet sister from interfering. Very special!

27

ARRIVAL OF MY
GRANDDAUGHTER IYLA

I HAD JUST RETURNED FROM ONE OF MY AMAZING TRAVELS. I WAS STILL VERY jet-lagged and tired and not sure what time of the day it was. Nevertheless, I cooked dinner and invited my son, David, and his girlfriend, Jenny, to dinner.

I was in the kitchen and concentrating on sautéing something, and it was not going the way I'd planned it. I was a bit frustrated, and my son came into the kitchen and wanted to show me something on his phone. I said, "Not right now," but he proceeded to show me anyway. I saw a picture of an ultrasound and a heartbeat, and then it dawned on me: it is a baby. Then he moved the ultrasound picture, and IT WAS JENNY! I managed to say something stupid: "Is it an oops baby?" And they both replied, "NO." My son disappointedly said that he expected me to be more excited about it. I was very tired, and my mind was hung up on the idea that events were not happening in the proper order. My OCD brain was going two hundred miles per hour. I feverishly tried to suggest some kind of small wedding, just immediate family, like on a boat or at Skamania Lodge, but to everything I suggested, my future daughter-in-law politely replied: "That's nice." I did not see any big enthusiasm, so I just dropped it. They were old enough to do what they saw as appropriate.

The pregnancy was uneventful. David and Jenny went to New York, and then upon their return, they got married (no ceremony). Jenny continued to work and teach yoga almost to the very end of her pregnancy. The baby's name was going to be Isaak (my son was convinced that it was a boy). Then we went to another ultrasound and surprise, surprise, it's a girl! In Judaic tradition, the first letter of the name has to be the same, and since the first option was Isaak, it had to start with an *I*. After some deliberation, they chose the name Iyla!

The due date was April 1, 2018, but I guess Iyla decided not to make an appearance on April Fool's Day. Later—and I mean exactly a week later— I got a call from my son, David, asking me to come to Northwest Portland (where they lived) and take their dog for a walk, as they were heading to the Good Samaritan hospital. No concerns. It would probably be a while, I thought.

It was a Sunday, Easter Sunday, and probably a full moon. I met them at the hospital first, and the place was packed with women giving birth. Jenny's parents and I were all in the room with her and David. (The good old times when you were able to be in a hospital room with people!) Jenny was making very slow progress. I took the dog for a walk to the park, and maybe thirty or forty minutes later, my son called.

I heard urgency and anxiety, and he asked me to come back as soon as possible, as Jenny was going into an emergency C-section. My heart was beating really fast, and I was very anxious now. When I got there, Jenny appeared rather uncomfortable, but the emergency C-section did not start until an hour later. Apparently, they were short on staff and operating rooms? David changed and went with Jenny. I walked to the small waiting area and, to take my mind off the worry, talked to a couple grandparents who just started telling me that they were awaiting their third grandchild and their daughter-in-law was in C-section surgery now.

At that time, I saw David storming by with his face bright red—a face that was saying, "Trouble." I rushed out and asked him what happened, and he just replied: "She is not breathing." Who? Mom? Baby? I followed him to the small room in the back and saw a rescue team working on a baby who was dark purple. The resuscitation team was from Randall Children's Hospital, and they were intubating our precious Iyla. She was not breathing at birth, as she aspirated meconium (a name for baby poop, which was in her lungs and caused pneumonitis).

I was a nervous wreck and talked to the pediatrician about potential long-term consequences. She showed me an x-ray and said that I knew that it is really hard to predict. Now Iyla was intubated and being moved to PICU (pediatric intensive care unit) at Randall Children's Hospital. For the first time in my life, I really wished that I was not a doctor and did not have all that body of knowledge! That knowledge was hurting me now!!!

We were all at the Randall Children's Hospital ICU watching our sweet Iyla wired up with all the tubing! She was being poked and probed. She was born a good size at 8.2 pounds and 20 inches long. The team intubated her, and the projection was for her to be in PICU for three to four weeks. Two different antibiotics were flowing into those tiny veins. After intubation, she had CPAP in three different sizes, etc. The picture was really grim.

My son, David, and I took a little break and went downstairs to the cafeteria to get something to drink. When we were downstairs in a long hallway, we passed by a glassed memorial garden. At that time, David looked up to the sky and in obvious desperation said, "Isaak, help me!" And almost in the same breath, he exclaimed, "It's a butterfly! Did you see it?" I did not, but he did. That butterfly was meant especially for him!

I can describe a lot of worries and heartaches in those five days. Yes, our little bundle of joy exceeded all expectations. She happens to be a fierce fighter. She pulled out essentially all her tubing and the most uncomfortable breathing device, CPAP, before it was taped down. Her oxygen saturation was at 100 percent on room air, and she went home after five days in the PICU! Our little fighter girl pushed forward to life, and that special butterfly was watching over her.

There were challenges with breastfeeding, and she was somewhat late in crawling, walking, and running, but she did it all. She is still slow on speech and talks selectively, but we all hope that her speech will blossom one day soon and we are probably not going to be able to stop her. She understands everything in two languages (Russian and English). She definitely knows what she wants and what she likes, and even without saying much, she almost always succeeds in conveying her message. She has her favorite music, favorite Disney movies, favorite characters. Through her I learned *Frozen*, *The Little Mermaid*, *The Lion King*, and *Aladdin*. I realized that before I only knew *Cinderella*.

Iyla is a joy of all our lives, that big-eyed girl who loves HUGS and kisses. She is going to be a very opinionated little girl, and I cannot wait to see it! May your special butterfly always watch over you!

28

MY MOST INCREDIBLE TRAVELS!

As I MENTIONED IN ANOTHER CHAPTER, I WAS LUCKY TO BE ABLE TO DO A LOT of travel, and travel became my savior. The experiences I had were so amazing that I decided to do a special summary chapter just on travel. And maybe, just maybe, in time my children and grandchildren will find it an interesting read? Honestly, right now they do not care much, but one day I hope they will.

This is just a brief summary, and I hope to avoid repeating other chapters. Not only is travel incredible in itself (seeing different places, learning about different cultures and people), but it also helps you to discover yourself—something about yourself that you did not know or maybe suspected but never uncovered until you traveled. Travel is certainly amazing, and like I said previously, I was really fortunate to be able to afford it and, unexpectedly, happen to have all the time in the world to do it.

So, pretty much since I left in January of 2013 for the most amazing journey to Antarctica, the Galápagos, and Machu Picchu, I continued to go for the next six or seven years. I am so glad that I did! Who knew that the world and travel would change so drastically in 2020?

One word to describe all my travels is *breathtaking*!!! I already told you how pristine and incredibly untouched the continent of Antarctica was in 2013! I loved those penguins and never have I seen so many and what good swimmers they are. I also learned that some of the most known and used medicines were studied on penguins (a good example being medicine for osteoporosis).

Then the Galápagos—what an incredible sanctuary for sea creatures and birds. Seals, sea lions, giant turtles, blue-footed boobies (birds), red crabs, and different types of fish that I'd never even heard about! I love how protected they all are at those islands. You cannot just decide to fly, backpack, and do your own things. Your visit has to be prearranged. Flights arrive only on certain days, and you can visit islands only on a charter boat. On our charter boat, I met a guy from San Diego who was circling the WORLD on his multimillion-dollar yacht. In the Galápagos, he and his girlfriend had to be on a charter boat in order to visit the islands. Watching hundreds and hundreds of seals and sea lions lying on the beach with their young (just born) was an incredible sight. Seeing blue-footed boobies for the first time?!

Machu Pichu—I was scheduled to go with Isaak in 2007, but that is when he finally was diagnosed with pulmonary fibrosis and we could not go. So, I had to finish that adventure and climb to the highest point (Sun Gate), three miles, in Isaak's memory.

The next year brought the incredible continent of Africa, with beautiful, incredible sights and proud, hardworking people. After my visit to Africa, I could not go to the zoo for a long time. Once you see those amazing creatures roaming freely on a safari, you cannot look at them in the zoo in cages.

Then was my incredible trip to Eastern Europe—Poland, Germany, Czech Republic, Hungary, and Croatia. When I lived in Ukraine (western Ukraine), I was a three-hour drive from Poland. Never could I dream of visiting Poland then! I also went on to Turkey to see ancient history and to sail for a week on an incredible boat in the pristine waters of the Mediterranean, eating catch of the sea prepared by the staff. All unforgettable experiences!

Then on to Iceland, and even though I did not see the Aurora/ northern lights, it was another absolutely unbelievable place and great culture!

Israel is an incredible, young country that was built on centuries and centuries of biblical history. Standing at the Western Wall always gives me the chills and a deep, indescribable feeling of an emotional high or emotional roller coaster! I've now been to Israel five times, and I always experience that at the wall!

Then visiting the Norwegian fjords and climbing the Preikestolen/Pulpit Rock (which I dreamed about for two years) was truly a dream come true!

And then the trip to Japan! Completely different and beautiful country and culture. People are polite and appear reserved, and as I learned, they have great insight and respect for other human beings. Oh, and their toilets? Do not even start me on that! Very interesting cultural experience!

It is a small but big world. So, I have been to every continent. In the USA I have traveled to twenty-seven states—I still have twenty-four to go. There are 195 countries in this world, and I have been to sixty-three of them. Still many more to visit! Travel is my happy place, and I hope to be able to return there soon!

29

STORY GOES ON...TRAVEL TO ITALY, MAY 2019

In 2019, a few friends and I decided to go on a Mediterranean cruise. It would be in May, and the cruise would sail from Civitavecchia, Italy (a small coastal suburb of Rome). When we scheduled the cruise, I decided that I also needed to see more of Italy. When Isaak and I had emigrated, we did come through Italy, and then we were fortunate to visit Italy a few times afterward. We both loved Italy and visited Rome a few times and also Florence, Venice, Pisa, Capri, and Pompeii! The last time that we were on a visit to Italy, I watched all those young people backpacking through Europe, and that always gave me a slightly euphoric, sweet sense of going into unknown exploring. I always wanted to do that. So, on Isaak's and my last visit, I suggested that sometime we should try that?! He told me that we were too old for that. So, in 2019 I decided that I was not too old and I would do just that!

I would do it all by myself, as my cruise companion was not able to take more time off (as she was still working). The solo adventure was amazing, and at the same time, I am glad that I did not leave everything to chance, did my homework, and made prior arrangements. I was really happy that I enlisted the help of a travel agent in purchasing train tickets, and even the trained travel agent had difficulty in arranging that with three different Italian companies and explaining tickets to me. If I had left that to chance, I would have had difficulty making connections, etc. Customer service as we know it here is essentially nonexistent in Italy. I also myself booked some hotels and some major tours that I wanted to do. That helped me to structure my tour a little bit.

My hotels were mostly hole-in-the-wall places, but they were close to train stations and main city attractions. That does not mean that I found them right away, but it was actually rewarding and a booster to my confidence when I finally was able to find them. You see, I am absolutely directionally impaired, and I had no GPS (but even if I did have it, it is not always helpful to me). So, I just stop random people and ask for help. I see that as a part of the cultural experience, and I love socializing with locals. Some are more receptive then others, some will just wave you away, but I looked at that as a learning experience nevertheless.

At the beginning of my trip, I flew to Milan, and from the airport I took a train to the stop in town that was supposed to be located eight minutes from my hole-in-the-wall hotel. I found it in two hours and thirty-eight minutes and saw some attractions at night, stopped a bunch of people, and asked for direction. Some did not speak English, so they just waved me away. Finally I stopped two young girls at a traffic circle (that I had been around three times by now) and asked if they spoke English, and they responded, "A little." Then one looked on her phone for a while, and then she said to her friend in Russian, "Maybe you look, as you're better with this than I am." There was no problem in communication then, and they finally helped me find my hotel! To me it's little moments like that that make the search so very memorable.

I did have two full-day tours booked, and the next morning I was off on a tour to see the famous Lake Como. I took a beautiful boat ride around the lake with all its incredible mansions and of course took probably one hundred pictures of George Clooney's home at the lake. Then all of a sudden we were caught in a torrential rain with hail at the end of the boat trip. We stopped at Bellagio and explored it in the rain and then had an incredible lunch and dried out in a very authentic restaurant! Everything was beautiful and amazing, and even rain could not spoil it for me! Of course, I am from Portland!

The next day I was on an all-day tour on the *Bernina Express* train that goes over the Alps to the beautiful Saint Moritz in Switzerland. What a great trip that was in a winter wonderland (going from eighty degrees to thirty-five in a matter of a few hours, from sunshine to snow). The scenery was unforgettable!

The next day was my last day in Milan, so now I needed to see Milan. I really wanted to see La Scala Theatre and not just a tour of the theater, but I was trying to see a performance. When I asked the hotel to look up what was playing at the theater, they just kept saying that I needed to go to the underground Metro and find a booth that sells tickets to La Scala. It was a Sunday, and I did not want to get lost in a rather complicated underground Metro. Even the young clerks in the hotel could not look it up for me. I guess they did not use Google? Anyway, I finally just asked them for directions to the theater, and they pointed in the general direction. I found La Scala by noon, and there was a performance at 2:00 p.m.

After navigating a maze of a ticket-buying adventure, I was finally inside and listening to the opera thinking how wonderful it would be to understand it. I was in the first row of the second balcony, and there was a Japanese girl on one side of me and Japanese guy on another side. In intermission not only did I explore the whole theater, but then I discovered that right in front of my seat was a translation device for every imaginable language. So in the second half of the opera, I caught up with the meaning of the play in two languages, English and Russian.

Then I was off to Duomo, Milan's beautiful cathedral. I was taking a picture when a guy brought me a rose. I wanted to pay, but he refused and said, "Just for you," but I paid anyway. Then I discovered Arco della Pace (Arc of Peace). It's a mecca for shoppers, but luckily I am not one!

The next morning, finding a connecting train was somewhat challenging but doable. I arrived in Venice, stepped out of the train, and I was in front of a canal and multiple kiosks. One guy in my hiking group from home had strongly suggested taking a vaporetto (basically a public water taxi, that takes you all through the canals). So I just bought a forty-eight-hour pass right there in one of those kiosks. I'm so glad that I did—it was a lifesaver.

As soon as I found my hotel (which was a former monastery), I dropped my bag in the room and decided to walk to the main attraction, Piazza San Marco, the city's main public square that contains its most famous buildings, such as Saint Mark's Basilica and Doge's Palace.

Piazza San Marco is in the heart of Venice. My guidebook said that the best way to see Venice was to get lost. I had no trouble doing just that. I wandered two or three hours through numerous small alleys and never knew where I was, and I made it to the plaza at dusk. The square looked so beautiful with lights! I explored the square, and then I realized that I was exhausted and probably would not find my way back. It was after ten p.m. I was grateful for buying that vaporetto ticket. I found it and was back to my hotel in thirty minutes.

The next day I cruised the canal and made it to the Grand Canal, Rialto Bridge, Doge's Palace (with a visit inside), Gallerie dell'Accademia, a memorial park/garden, the Jewish quarters with amazing food, and much more. I had an absolutely incredible time.

Then I was off on a train to Florence for three days in that magnificent city with (of course) an incredible cathedral and museums on every corner. I had an incredible time exploring Uffizi Gallery, Accademia Gallery (home to the Michelangelo's *David* and many other great sculptures). Art on every corner! The next two days were full-day tours. Tuscany wine country with a stop at a winery for lunch and wine. Then on to see Pisa, Siena, San Gimignano, and Lucca. It was a breathtaking tour with amazing scenery—incredible—and of course good food. The other tour was by bus, train, and boat to the amazing Cinque Terre (five beautiful villages built into the side of a cliff). Incredibly colorful, and each one had its own flavor of food. There I met my neighbor (who I barely see in Portland). And then I was on to Rome. I met my friend, and we did a half-day morning tour of the Vatican and then went on foot to the Colosseum, the Pantheon, the Trevi Fountain, the Sistine Chapel, Saint Peter's Basilica, II Vittoriano (including the Tomb of the Unknown Soldier), Piazza Navona, and the Spanish Steps. We literally walked through Rome. No taxi, no bus, just walked to exhaustion to see all those beautiful sites!

From Rome we went on to Naples with its rather beautiful downtown fortress. This is the place of the first pizza, but we did not like it much. On the other hand, dessert was superb and delicious. Naples was my jumping-off point to the Amalfi Coast and Ravello and Positano. What incredible scenery! Back to Rome, and the next morning we took another train to Civitavecchia and off on our Mediterranean cruise.

That was a lot of fun. More of beautiful Italy with its all-white stone villages, along with Barcelona, Spain; Marseille, France; Monte Carlo, Monaco; and other incredible places! Then we returned to Rome to see some neighborhoods at night, which was a lot of fun. The next day was our last day in Rome, and I suggested to my roommate that we visit Ladispoli (a small suburban town where Isaak and I had spent a month being "processed" on our way to the USA, and the same for my friend). She was tired and not sure if she wanted to do it. She finally agreed, and there we were on our way down my memory lane! After learning yet another system of purchasing tickets, we are on a forty-minute ride to Ladispoli. We arrived around four o'clock. It had been thirty-nine years for me and twenty-nine years for her! She was thrilled to be there as she remembered much more. She exclaimed: "Cannot you remember? Here was the market and there was kids carousel." She pointed to a carousel that was still there. I only remember the fountain with benches around it? She later told me that that was a highlight of her trip!?

I feel incredibly lucky and fortunate that I was able to do it all! Who knows if we will ever be able to do it again!

I am strongly convinced that if it's possible, we should live the dream! Today and now, as tomorrow is not guaranteed!

30

HOW THE WHOLE WORLD SUDDENLY CHANGED! COVID-19, 2020

I HAD JUST RETURNED FROM A BEAUTIFUL CRUISE WITH A FRIEND TO ALL THE Hawaiian Islands! The year was 2020, January. We had a great time cruising from San Francisco to Hawaii and dancing our nights away before, during, and after the New Year! We met some great people and just enjoyed our time of fifteen days on *Grand Princess*.

My general rule is when I am away on vacation, I am away from everything, and normally I do not listen to the news or check emails. So I am really away and enjoying the moment. When I returned, I began to hear more about that mysterious infection from Wuhan, China, seriously affecting and killing a lot of people! Well, we had SARS and H1N1 and others. My initial feeling was that this too shall pass!

I remember that day like it was yesterday. I had just completed a bridge walk with my Meetup group, and we were in downtown Portland at the market having lunch. My daughter called (at a rather unusual time of the day), and I could tell immediately from her voice that something had happened, and I questioned her. She replied that she debated whether to tell me or not, but then she did not want me to hear it from local or national news, and she went on to tell me that Chad—my son-in-law who is an emergency room doctor in Washington—had just had a number of patients from a long-term care facility coming to his emergency room for the virus and on to the ICU, being intubated, and one of them died! There was lots of confusion at that time as to what that mysterious illness was, who had taken care of whom, suspicions about the new virus that not much was known about, etc. It was on the news, and yes, it was quickly the number one cause of mortality in the USA, and from that time on, I did not stop worrying about the safety of my children, grandchildren, and extended family.

For a whole long month I worried about Chad's safety, about his personal protection, the safety of the family in contact with him (and for a while, they all separated themselves as a precaution and lived on different levels of the house). Did his hospital have enough protective equipment? Was that equipment sufficient? The CDC announced that we were in a pandemic. Horrible pictures from New York, the death rate staggering (I lost a relative my age in New York to COVID). Then awful pictures and videos from Italy—ambulances and sirens through the most beautiful places that I'd walked through less than a year ago?

The snowball kept rolling, and we could not downplay what a horrible monster the whole world was fighting now. Then children's schools closed, and everything became virtual. No school sports or any socializing of any kind. Then the major leagues closed down too. No symphonies, outdoor concerts, or blues festivals. No theater and no annual trip to Ashland's Shakespeare Festival. Restaurants closing temporarily or going out of business. I am sure that you are getting it (we are all still living it now!!!!).

Nobody in the medical communities really knew how invasive and unpredictable this virus was. There were conflicting reports, lots of disagreements among different groups on social media. We saw families break apart over that. People became more withdrawn, isolated, afraid, anxious. The fear of the unknown is a great one! I was still helping out with my granddaughter, who was almost two, and one day my daughter called from Seattle and told me that I really should not be doing it, as kids can be vectors for the disease even if they're asymptomatic. In the middle of February, I left my son's home and shortly after, we all went into quarantine. Medical experts were guessing two weeks, maybe two months? Experts debated, and different theories rolled out. The borders closed, shutting down the travel industry as many other industries went up in smoke. Many experienced bankruptcy, unemployment, and the effects of a stock market crash.

I do not know by what miracle, but I did get on Zoom. Our whole lives revolve around Zoom now! At about a month into quarantine, and in spite of Zoom and FaceTime, I began to bitterly miss seeing my grandkids. I needed a hug, and I wanted to give them lots of hugs! I decided to drive to Seattle to see my children (in spite of Chad, the front-line worker, not being convinced that it was a good idea). My grandkids Michael and Anne were growing up too fast, and I so missed seeing them.

I can tell you that I have done the trip from Portland to Seattle hundreds if not thousands of times, but this one was the eeriest experience. There was not another car from Oregon on the road! They were mostly from Washington, some California, Idaho, and other states. Not a single other car with Oregon license plates? It felt like I could be arrested for trespassing. I finally arrived, and we had so much fun together eating takeout in the park around the lake in Kirkland and walking around the lake all together with their dog, Kobe (who never fails to bark at me first and then becomes my best friend). I'd missed my children and our togetherness. Life—at least for those few days—felt normal like the "good old times."

Then I returned to Portland, and I wanted to see my other granddaughter Iyla in person (not on FaceTime). At almost two years old, she did not get the concept of Zoom or FaceTime. So, I went to their neighborhood, and we agreed to meet and stay on opposite sides of the street, all with masks. We met, and I was probably ten feet away from them. My baby was seeing her *baba* (Russian for "grandma"), who had previously spent three to four days a week with her ever since she was born, and she of course ran to me. My son scooped her and said, "No." The child was very confused. What was going on? We were all confused. Life was not even making sense anymore. Then to top it off, my daughter-in-law made an announcement that they were expecting another child, and all I could say was "Now?" Of course she told me that all of that was planned in that other "normal world." I was happy but also very confused...

I began to see people I knew lose their lives to that horrible virus, and others got very ill and for a long time from it. I saw divisions in families, and isolation and depression and anxiety all added to that! Our world deeply changed! This virus is very peculiar and unpredictable, and it's been over a year now and it keeps changing! We still have a lot to learn, and unfortunately it looks like we are in for a long haul with it.

It was rather sad to see that, after playgrounds finally opened and Iyla, a complete hugger like her baba, went and tried to hug kids on the playground, some of them cried bitterly, as they'd lost or never had the knowledge of a hug. Sad, very sad. I hope and pray that we can get back to hugging each other. It's a basic need for human touch.

I also really hope that we will get our beautiful country back, the one we came to for freedom! I also hope and pray that this world will be healed not only from that nasty virus but from other ugliness and diseases that came with that time. Hopefully, we can travel again and explore this beautiful land and all live in good health, harmony, and peace.

31

MY ANCESTORS ARE
WATCHING OVER ME

I HAVE ARRIVED AT THE CONCLUSION—YOU MAY SAY THE GREAT FINALE—OF my book. And it's dedicated to ALL the beautiful, warm, witty, delightful people who I came from and lived with, and who made me into who I am today!

They all contributed and molded me like clay. My big tribute and loving bow to all of them.

My grandpa Itzhak Iosifovich Gendler, that very meticulous, smart, deeply religious man played a very pivotal role in my upbringing, probably more vital to my personality then he ever suspected. He passed on when I was fourteen years old, and even though he refused to teach me about Judaism, he planted a seed. I developed deep appreciation and curiosity as well as a desire to learn and study about it. Every year when I say a Kaddish (a memorial prayer for the departed on the anniversary of their death) for my grandpa, I think that he is watching me from heaven and rejoicing! He also (maybe without even knowing it) taught me how to love fellow men/women no matter what their affiliation, religion, skin color, status in society, wealth, or appearance, etc. He taught me to not get angry with people, but if I do, better to wish them well than to swear and use bad words. He was my own Dalai Lama.

But he also was human and made mistakes, for which he paid dearly. He took the secret to his grave!

My dearest grandmother Khasya Lazarevna Grosman, our matriarch of the family, my friend, so smart and beautiful and erudite! She was fearless and had great insight, was able to read people and taught me that. Thanks to Grandma, I met the love of my life, Isaak, and before I knew it, she told me (just as she was watching me open a letter from him) that he was going to be my husband. And he was for an amazing forty years! My grandma apparently was very shrewd in matters of the heart. She was very special! She, too, was human and made some bitter mistakes, for which she paid dearly! She also took the family secrets to her grave. I am only imagining how difficult it was for her not to share them with anybody and how stoic she was to shield me from the truth, even though it had been known to others.

My parents Anna and Mikhail Chernobelsky. I miss them both very much—their love and their care, dedication to us children, hugs and kisses, and of course, my mom's cooking and advice... It's been so many years since they left this world, but I still feel them sometimes hovering over me and my children. I almost feel their presence. I still think sometimes, *What would my mom say to that?*

Mom, I sure hope that you have a great kitchen in heaven, and I know that you will find people to feed and I know that they would love it!

Dad, your love and affection turned me into a complete hugger, and this year it was hard because of COVID-19. But I continue to hug my children as per your teaching—life is not worth living if you cannot hug. I carry your warmth in my heart.

My beautiful hummingbird (who I know carries both your spirits) very frequently hovers over me for a long time, just like you did in life! So, I know that you are watching over me and continue to protect me.

And of course, my husband, my dearest loving Isaak! Oh, how much I miss you!!! It has been over eight long years since you left this world at such a young age, way too soon. You, my love, your great spirit, your deep unwavering love for me and the family, will always remain with us! We miss you so much! I come to visit you at the cemetery often and tell you everything about all of us but especially about our children and grandchildren that you cherished so much.

You loved Anne and Michael beyond any measure, and they were seven and nine when you slipped away into your medical coma. I tell you what awesome young adults they are becoming, and I know that you are smiling from heaven. Our little Annie is a young lady of almost sixteen, and every time I see her picture, I ask Lils, "Who is that beautiful young lady next to you???" She is beautiful and smart and lovable! Michael just turned eighteen and has been accepted to Northwestern University in Chicago. I am very proud of him, and I know that you are too.

You unfortunately did not meet David's kids (yes, *kids*, plural). You know about them, as I know you do! Iyla is named for you, and she is sweet and witty and knows to give me *Golovochku* (Russian for "head," where you liked to kiss our grandkids). In November she became a big sister, as Jenny and David had another girl by the name of Gemma Grace, who is the sweetest smiling girl, and the big sister loves and hugs her all the time. I soooo wish you could share that joy with me. But I know that you do!

Love and miss you forever, my love!

My two uncles Josef and Lazar Gendler, who died during WWII in their teens, way too soon—I remember you every year in my memorial prayers, along with multiple other cousins, aunts and uncles, grandaunts, my parents-in-law, and other relatives. All of you are on another side that we don't know or understand, but I choose to believe that each one of you is sending one speck of a particle to communicate with me and, yes, to watch over all of us.

Epilogue

FAMILY TREE/CHERRY TREE

MY GRANDPARENTS LIVED IN ODESSA, UKRAINE, THE BEAUTIFUL RESORT town by the Black Sea. They had a nice home with a very big cherry tree. Every summer that tree brought those delicious dark and juicy cherries. I loved them. I spent every summer at my grandparents' house, and very often you would find me at that tree eating those delicious cherries. My grandpa made cherry wine, and even as a young teenager, I was allowed a taste of it, and it was so good!

Then many years later I was in the beautiful country of the USA, our new and only home! Our son, David, married a very special girl, Jenny, and she is the daughter of cherry farmers.

We all love cherries. Then Iyla was born and loves all fruits, and of course she loves cherries. She also loves tractors and horses. Then in November 2020, Gemma Grace was born and my daughter, Lilya, and her two awesome kids, my amazing grandkids, came to meet their new cousin. Michael and Anne came to celebrate Gemma's arrival, and we toasted Gemma's arrival with a cherry liqueur that I'd brought from Japan four years before!

I do not buy anything when I travel anymore, but that time when I was tasting that cherry liqueur in Japan (which is apparently the favorite of the emperor of Japan), I was thinking of my grandpa's cherry wine. So I bought that bottle and a butterfly ring. Both I needed to have!

So that cherry tree from my childhood made a full circle in my life, and it just so happens that it tied us all together through generations—activities, travel, ancestors, and our future, the next generation.

The cherry tree has become my family tree.

ACKNOWLEDGMENTS

First of all, I would like to acknowledge my wonderful family, who provided their support and encouragement for writing this book, who believed in me and gave me a helpful hand on the darkest of my days. This book is a labor of love, and without you and your love, it would have been impossible to bring to completion.

Thank you to my extended family, my brother and his family, who helped me to decode the mysterious puzzles of well-kept family secrets. Those occasional clues are what, with time, raised my curiosity and made me dig deeper and deeper for answers.

Thank you, Michael, for telling me that you would read my book! That in itself was a great encouragement for writing and finishing the book. Thank you, Anne, for agreeing to help me with typing (you are obviously a much better typist), and even though it did not happen because of COVID, your offer was very meaningful to me and a boost to my confidence. Always proud of you!

To Jenny, my daughter-in-law, who did type one chapter for me in spite of being a busy mom and a working woman.

Thank you to those in my family who have left this world and taught me an incredible lesson on self-sacrifice! I am sure that it was very hard. Forgive me for not asking you when I could!

I need to say thank you to my memoir class instructor at Portland Community College, Jenny Forrester, who showed me that anyone could be a writer. My first formal look at memoir writing. To Ali Shaw, who picked up that torch and carried it very proudly and with great knowledge. I learned a lot in your amazing workshops! From the moment I saw you in Jenny's memoir class and asked you a few questions, I knew that you are not just an absolutely wonderful person but also very knowledgeable and understanding and caring. So glad that our paths crossed. Thank you for the reading that you organized at Beaverton City Library, where I had absolute strangers come up and encourage me to write!

To my classmates Maggie, Ali, Margo, Basha, Shavaun, Lisa, Dawn, and Sydney (Syd), who shared their beautiful stories and listened to mine.

And last but not least to Ali Shaw, editor, and all the beautiful people at Indigo: Editing, Design, and More for your support, guidance, and patience. Without you, this book would not be possible. Thank you, thank you, thank you.

ABOUT THE AUTHOR

RAISA PREMYSLER is a retired physician who is residing in the beautiful Pacific Northwest. She is not a writer by trade and has no other publications.

This memoir is a huge labor of love and dedication. Raisa considers it an ethical will to her children. She would be happy to answer questions or receive comments about it at ipremysler@yahoo.com.

Premysler

FAMILY SCRAPBOOK

Grandma Khasya

Grandpa Itzhak

Mom, Anya Chernobelsky

Dad, Mikhail Chernobelsky

*My grandmother (middle), mother (right), my brother (left),
me (front), and family friends*

Me as a snowflake in kindergarten

Me in my twenties, looking similar
to the woman in Garry Winogrand's famous photograph

Isaak and his dad

Isaak in uniform

Isaak and me at our wedding

Isaak and our
daughter, Lilya

Lilya

Isaak and our
son, David

Grandma Khasya and David

*Sibling love,
hopefully forever*

Me, David, Lilya, and Isaac—Isaak's favorite photo

Meeting Elie Wiesel at Linfield College

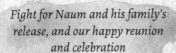

*Fight for Naum and his family's
release, and our happy reunion
and celebration*

Family good times in the park, 1989 or 1990

Mom's seventy-fifth birthday celebration

Reconciliation and forgiveness

Building a dream

Family Thanksgiving 2018

Lilya's wedding: Me, Lilya, and my mom

*Isaak and Lilya for the
father-daughter dance*

*My brother, Naum, and my nephew
waiting to take Mom down the aisle at
Lilya's wedding*

*My mom and
Naum's kids*

My brother, Naum, and his wife

Our daughter's family

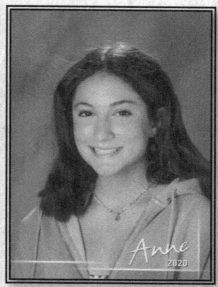

Anne

Michael

Michael and Baba
(me, Russian for "Grandmother")

Isaak and me with Michael and Anne

Our daughter's family

Our three grandkids and a furry grandchild

Iyla's baby naming ceremony

Our son's family

Iyla

Our son's family

Iyla's first birthday

Gemma

Iyla and her mom

Iyla and Gemma

Our son's family

Isaak and me on our first trip
to Israel and the Dead Sea

Isaak at Monument Valley, Arizona

Isaak in Israel

Isaak and me at Iguazu Falls in South America

Travel became my savior! Me at Machu Picchu, Peru